PRAISE FOR *GRACE POINTS*

"This book will provide consolation and hope for its readers as they search for meaning in their life situations. With warmth and compassion radiating from her own desert transition experiences, the author chronicles the wilderness wanderings familiar to many of us. The challenge to become more than survivors, and the reality that we can flourish and grow during our desert passages, will prove to be an epiphany for many readers. The 'Grace Points' will help readers find quietness, peace and strength as they reflect on their journeys, search their souls and develop intimacy with their God."

DR. FREDA V. CREWS, HOST OF *TIME FOR HOPE*
AND LICENSED PROFESSIONAL COUNSELOR

"If you are dealing with transitions and change, *Grace Points* is the book for you! Jane Rubietta skillfully weaves personal stories with biblical truth, while gently encouraging the reader not to run from the pain of transition. You will learn how to hear God's voice in the wilderness of change. This book is equally effective for personal or small group study. Don't miss it!"

CAROL KENT, PRESIDENT, SPEAK UP SPEAKER SERVICES

In *Grace Points*, Jane Rubietta moves us toward key life choices, which she honestly portrays from her own life. I found myself longing for more of God's grace and being delighted when heaven covered me with it. You'll laugh, weep, reflect and act on timeless truths that, when embraced, bring purpose and fulfillment. Savor it in a measured and thoughtful manner, as I have."

GAIL MACDONALD, AUTHOR OF *HIGH CALL, HIGH PRIVILEGE*
AND *IN HIS EVERLASTING ARMS*

"*Grace Points* is *the* book for anyone in a life change, transition or crisis; for anyone who has been through a life change, transition or crisis; or for anyone who will go through a life change, transition or crisis. In other words, *Grace Points* is a must-read for everyone who wants to go through a life transition and come out better on the other side."

PAM FARREL, AUTHOR OF *WOMAN OF INFLUENCE*,
WOMAN OF CONFIDENCE AND *MEN ARE LIKE WAFFLES*,
WOMEN ARE LIKE SPAGHETTI

"Instead of viewing major transitions in our lives as unwelcome intruders, Jane Rubietta encourages us to be still, reflect and grow from our times of uncertainty. Transitions seem to place us in a barren wilderness, but God is Lord of the wilderness, and it is there that we can experience his transforming grace. *Grace Points* is an excellent 'wilderness survival' guidebook filled with wisdom, personal insights, relevant Scripture, well-chosen hymns and response questions to help us embrace the blessings and growth that only wilderness times can give."

CYNTHIA HEALD, AUTHOR OF *BECOMING A WOMAN OF EXCELLENCE*

GRACE

POINTS

Growth and Guidance in Times of Change

Jane Rubietta

InterVarsity Press
Downers Grove, Illinois

InterVarsity Press
P.O. Box 1400, Downers Grove, IL 60515-1426
World Wide Web: www.ivpress.com
E-mail: mail@ivpress.com

InterVarsity Press® *is the book-publishing division of InterVarsity Christian Fellowship/USA*®, *a student movement active on campus at hundreds of universities, colleges and schools of nursing in the United States of America, and a member movement of the International Fellowship of Evangelical Students. For information about local and regional activities, write Public Relations Dept., InterVarsity Christian Fellowship/USA, 6400 Schroeder Rd., P.O. Box 7895, Madison, WI 53707-7895, or visit the IVCF website at <www.ivcf.org>.*

All Scripture quotations, unless otherwise indicated, are taken from the Holy Bible, New International Version®. NIV®. *Copyright* ©1973, 1978, 1984 by International Bible Society. Used by permission of Zondervan Publishing House. All rights reserved.

"Word" by Madeleine L' Engle is reprinted from Penguins and Golden Calves. Copyright © 1996 and 2003 by Crosswicks, Ltd. Used by permission of Waterbrook Press, Colorado Springs, CO. All rights reserved.

Cover design: Cindy Kiple

Cover image: Birgit Utech/Photonica

ISBN 0-8308-1952-5

Printed in the United States of America ∞

Library of Congress Cataloging-in-Publication Data

Rubietta, Jane.
  Grace points: growth and guidance in times of change / Jane
  Rubietta.
    p. cm.
Includes bibliographical references.
  ISBN 0-8308-1952-5 (pbk.: alk paper)
  1. Christian women—Prayer-books and devotions-English. 2.
Change—Prayer-books and devotions—English. I. Title.
  BV4844.R83 2004
  248.4—dc22

                                                                        2003020591

P	17	16	15	14	13	12	11	10	9	8	7	6	5	4	3	2	1
Y	16	15	14	13	12	11	10	09	08	07	06	05	04				

For the writers in my life:

Lynn Austin, Joy Bocanegra, Lin Johnson and Cleo Lampos,

beloved friends who have both shaped and shared

my journey in the wilderness of change;

and for my sister, Sara Kelley,

whose grace, compassion and laughter point me to the Lord.

CONTENTS

Introduction

𝒯he Mojave Desert stretches for miles under our plane. Browns and red-brown, hundreds of shades of dirt. Crusty brown, flaky brown, sandy brown. Dry snakes of etchings where water once ran. Tall, flat, hilly . . . endless variations on a long, dry theme. The Mojave seems an appropriate image to depict our wide variety of transitions, our life changes.

Occasionally a community perches on the dirt, tentative but tenacious to plant itself in the midst of the barrenness. Trees hunker up next to the towns, protectively. The desert creeps to the edges of the outlying yards, grass and sand defying one another for turf rights. Tiny roads inscribed into the palm of the desert underscore the routes of an occasional auto.

The wilderness is not densely populated it would appear. Harsh living situations and extreme conditions deem it a pass-through necessity. But not home. Instead, the desert is a forming place, a shaping instrument, a school of sorts where we learn who we are and where we are going. But we are transients, each in transition, on the way to our ultimate home, and so we trek on.

When I arrived at the LA airport prior to my departure for Chicago, the cushion of time felt comfortable. Until I saw a line of luggageless people, long enough to wrap around a high school track a couple of times. The shuttle driver groaned and mumbled about the crowd, and I looked in alarm at my watch. "Don't worry. They're all going to Las Vegas for the day," he said. "They can get a cheap same-day rate out of here, so before dawn they wait in line to buy their tickets. First come, first serve."

So many people try to miss transition's desert—fleeing any pain or anxiety in transition by spending their way out, whether spending time,

money, affection or energy. Whatever ticket it takes to get us out of the
guts of change and thinking about something, anything, else.

Rather than trying to flee from the changes, in *Grace Points* we will try
to stay with our heart in the middle of the changes affecting our life.
Grace Points is designed to be a tool to anchor us to God and to our soul
in times of change, providing both growth and guidance in our journey.
Incorporated into the structure of each chapter are places for us to slow
down, digest, wait on our heart as we unearth wilderness feelings.

GETTING THE MOST FROM *GRACE POINTS*

Still Points. Opening each chapter with a principle thought of stillness
in the whirling chaos of our transitioning, this meditative quote is intended to slow us down and move us toward God.

Travelogue. Throughout each chapter are memory points, places
where we take out our journals and take note of what our heart is saying
to us, what our emotions are telling us, what God's Spirit is whispering
to us. These notes will guide us as we remember where we have been,
giving us hope for where we are heading.

Wilderness Response. An application section closes each chapter,
including:

• *Accompaniment Psalm.* This Scripture selection brings us into
God's heart, inviting us to meditate on the connection between the chapter subject and God's Word to us, God's track record with both the Israelites and with us.

• *Desert Reading.* A passage, typically from the Old Testament, sharing more of the Israelites' journey through their own wilderness of
transition, out of Egypt and toward the Promised Land. Here we might
ask ourselves who God is in the passage and how our situations fit into
the story.

• *Guiding Song.* These are traditional hymns with deep words, moving us into a place of contemplation. You don't have to sing or even know
the melody; the words can be read as you would read poetry, slowly,

thoughtfully, inviting the Lord's grace and healing into your heart.

• *Remember Your Journey.* This is the take-home section, beckoning us to put our hand into God's for the next leg of the trip, to journal about particular places of contact with our pain, with our Lord, with others.

SMALL GROUP SUGGESTIONS

Like the desert, transitions are best traveled with companions. The sections throughout each chapter are designed for use in personal reflection and meditation as well as in small groups, and they are easily facilitated even without having an official leader. The thought starters in "Travelogue" as well as "Remember Your Journey" allow facilitators to incorporate key points of the subject into areas of discussion and application. Using *Grace Points* in a small group setting allows women in all seasons of change a safe and structured place to share their typically personal transitions, loosen their "I'm fine" masks, and find support and grace en route. Questions can be used for discussion, for prayer points, and for application and accountability.

"Accompaniment Psalm" and "Desert Reading" Scriptures could be read aloud slowly, perhaps at both the beginning and the ending of the session. Group members may wish to close their eyes and listen for God's Word to speak to them in new and powerful ways, relating their specific seasons of change to the timeless truth and comfort of Scripture. The "Guiding Song" could be read aloud as poetry or sung in the group, making a fitting closing to the time together. The hymns are found in most hymnals for those who might prefer instrument accompaniment.

Whatever your place in life's journey, there is grace to help in times of need. May you find God's presence to be your richest companion as you travel through *Grace Points*.

Still Point

WORD

I, who live by words, am wordless when

I try my words in prayer. All language turns

To silence. Prayer will take my words and then

Reveal their emptiness. The stifled voice learns

To hold its peace, to listen with the heart

To silence that is joy, is adoration.

The self is shattered, all words torn apart

In this strange patterned time of contemplation

That, in time, breaks time, breaks words, breaks me,

And then, in silence, leaves me healed and mended.

I have returned to language, for I see

Through words, even when all words are ended,

I, who live by words, am wordless when

I turn me to the Word to pray.

Amen.

MADELEINE L'ENGLE

I
....

TRANSITIONS AND THE
WILDERNESS RESPONSE

For of His fullness we have all received, and grace upon grace.

JOHN 1:16 NASB

*A*round the table, coffee cups filled and emptied, chips disappeared, tears appeared, praise and back-clapping erupted, pain spilled. Since 1992, we four women have circled a table every month, and every month some new cliffhanger lands between us. We talk, support, eat, moan, roar with laughter and pray together. We are also professional mentors to one another, so sometimes we discuss work.

In all these years, the four of us have been unable to exit the cloverleaf of change. Almost every type of transition on the charts has been verbalized through our clenched teeth and then carried by one another. Kids married, children off to college, a painful divorce, serious illnesses, a college degree, new jobs, tragedies in extended families, vocational success and failure, moves, a change in life calling. Once, at a work-related retreat, Anne heaved a huge sigh and smiled. "Now. My kids are married, and their crises are their own. Now it's our time—time for our marriage, our life together." The next day, her daughter was rushed to the hospital with a medical trauma that nearly claimed her life. Anne's pulse didn't return to normal for years.

Our conclusion from these years of keeping tabs on one another: the type of change rotates, and sometimes the roller coaster flattens out, but the ride never ends. Occasionally the hills are thrilling, and others feel like a free fall from a water tower. The changes are ongoing until finally we shoot across that final river through the dark and into heaven.

The heaven part sounds good. The rest of it? Learning how not to white-knuckle our way through the ride. Learning how, and where, to find joy and grace in times of change, and how to transmit that to others. Learning how to live—really live—in the turmoil of transitions.

Sound like a page from your story? Welcome to life's perennial drama.

THE WILDERNESS FEELING

Wilderness. An untamed place. Uncultivated, barren, desertlike. Uninhabited, devoid of human beings. Uncharted territory. Swirling snow or blowing sand. Stinging cold or broiling heat. A land of extremes, of lostness, of endless horizons stretching God only knows where.

All are impressions we might associate with transitions. Loneliness and isolation compound the deserted feeling. Yet though our journeys are each individual, we are not alone or without role models in these desert treks. The Israelites knew the wilderness, knew life on the lam. When they moved in a time of famine to Egypt, their tiny nation enjoyed favorable treatment by the ruling Pharaoh, who had set up the Hebrew patriarch, Joseph, as second-in-command of the country. But times changed, the nation multiplied exponentially, and four hundred years later, the rulers had forgotten Joseph, forgotten their debt to the Israelites.

Threatened by the sheer numbers of Hebrews, Egypt enforced brutal slave labor, fearing an uprising. God, however, heard his people's cries for deliverance and with mighty power delivered them from the Egyptian rulers (Exodus 1:1—15:21). After running for their lives from slavery, they logged forty years of experience with transition as they followed God to the Promised Land (rehearsed by Moses in Deuteronomy 1:1—3:29). Their wilderness journeys will inform our travels as we work through our options in times of change.

TRANSITION'S TERRITORIES

Looking at categories of transitions helps identify our particular territory. Consider life changes for self or loved ones in any of these areas:

- a rearrangement in family relationships (birth, adoption, death, divorce, marriage, empty nest, boomerang kids, parent care, nursing home)
- health (our own or that of a loved one)
- life stage
- social relationships (friends, coworkers, church family, community relationships and involvements)
- work (job loss or change, downsizing, promotion, demotion, change in pay or benefits or colleagues, retirement)
- relocation (new home in the same community or in a new community)
- change in church community, structure, location, pastor/staff leadership
- ideology, worldview or spirituality

Life realignments, even positive ones, exact their toll on us.

THE WILDERNESS OF TRANSITION

Life shifts occur, making us feel as though the plates beneath the ground have grumbled and erupted in earthquake-sized trauma. Or perhaps they don't register on the Richter scale of human emotion; rather, a ripple here and there pushes us out of predictability and security. Change doesn't always feel drastic, or even desertlike. Change may even be welcome—the new job you wanted, the longed-for baby, the move into the house of your dreams. We forget that good transitions cost our systems energy and weigh on our spirits just as difficult life changes do.

Jim and Char, in their seventies, live on social security and little else.

TRAVELOGUE

• *Which of the specific*

transitions have you experienced

in the past five years or do you

anticipate in the next few years?

(You may identify more than one.)

• *What feelings or senses have you*

associated with transitions?

A small fixed income and looming medical problems leave them in fear. Pauline is a new mother and running into her own insufficiency and the firing/retiring of hormones. There is not enough of her to cover all the bases. She wonders if she made a mistake.

For Therese, whose husband lost his job and morale a year ago, life is a grim firefight with her own dreams and needs burned up in the blaze of overwork and over-compensation. With her toddler's diagnosis of brain cancer, Barb's world turned upside down. Disruption in Freda's church devastated her; now in a different church, she doesn't understand the subtle ache and underlying depression. Susan's empty nest after raising three children finds her disoriented, less organized and without energy to re-sort priorities.

With eleven moves in fifteen years, I considered myself an expert on change—until God called us from the local pastorate into a missionary type of position, where we lost 100 percent of salary, benefits and housing allowance and our expenses tripled. As our world of security rocked in the storm of such drastic change, God eventually took me into a deeper place of trust. But not without enormous wrestling with him, worry, sleeplessness and stress on my part, along with extreme overwork for both my husband and me as we tried to make certain we had a house to live in and food to eat. The strain deeply affected our family of five, as well as our extended family, as we tried to lash the sides of our lives together.

Transition's side effects are often unnoticed in the sandstorm of change, until a vague malaise, a "what's wrong with me?" fog drapes over us. Eventually we find ourself shaking sand out of our shoes, and we realize we're in the outback. There stress, anxiety, locked-in emotions and loss of sleep may buckle our flimsy tents. Whether transitions produce seismic shifts or sand in our teeth, they tax our emotional, spiritual and physical resources. Then it's time to add up the changes and look for grace, for that unmerited presence and favor of God in the midst of our desert.

THE WILDERNESS CHANGE

A group of long-trusted friends and I graphed the decades of our lives on life charts. We plotted high points above the line, hard times below. Looking at my clusters of peaks and swoops, my heart bumped in my chest. The points bulldozing the bottom were also the times that I felt God's presence and power had been the most dramatic. Those were the places where, in spite of my tears and fear and anguish, God established an incredible track record of faithfulness.

Very spiritual people have said this, to my annoyance and frank disbelief. It's a gift of retrospect, possibly, and as much as I have disliked hearing this from others, those hard and desperate plot points shaped my faith and changed me. Realizing this, I felt the confirmation of God's vital surrounding love and grace, even while venturing through this current wasteland of transition.

THE WILDERNESS LUGGAGE

Amy Tan's *The Joy Luck Club* opens with a description of a path on which hundreds of exiles trod. Remnants litter the roadside: discarded furniture, family treasures, items too big or bulky or cumbersome to carry. The road, much longer than they anticipated; the baggage, much heavier than they could haul.

Seasoned desert travelers pack lightly. They carry as little as possible in order to conserve energy while trudging through the scorching days, but they pack enough to sustain them in the cold nights. Needs are simple: water, food, protection from the elements and wildlife. If only we knew when exactly our feet touched the edges of the wilderness, if only the map were drawn a little more clearly and to scale, we could know what to pack in our duffels. As it is, too often we lift up our heads from our hike and realize, suddenly, that sand surrounds us; had we known our trip pointed us toward transition's wilderness, we could have prepared more thoroughly for the journey.

Still, recognizing this place of life change, this leg of our nomadic expedition, we can begin shedding extraneous baggage: peripheral involvements that exhaust or dislocate our gifts and goals, nagging duties that, in the final analysis, are optional and always draining. The wilderness is no time to heft extra weight. When someone asks, "Wouldn't you love to serve on this committee?" we can deprogram the default setting on our guilt-o-meter. The wilderness may not be the place for new responsibilities.

THE WILDERNESS LONGING

Inescapably, times of change eventually create longing: for protection, for security, for safe passage. We want comfort, sameness. We want our own bed! Transitions force the question: In what will we trust? Where will we find our hope when the world falls away from us, when the landscapes of our life are blurred by our tears, by sleepless eyes, and our nights haunted by doubts, misgivings and the specter of fear?

The desert also unveils a profound, piercing ache: all these longings and questions can be satisfied at their deepest level only by the presence of God.

And that is the grace point of transition.

THE WILDERNESS GIFT

In the midst of sorting through our longings and luggage, our insecurities and fears, when we're in danger of losing our bearings and perspective, forgetting where we're headed and why, remember: the instability, fragility and tenuous nature of life characterize each of us, regardless of life stage or age. None of us lives in stasis, in unchange.

No one, that is, but God. In God there is no changing. Immutable is our God. Our change becomes a chance to rely on the God who doesn't change but instead changes us. And so, even in times of great shaking, where all our familiar structures appear to be shifting, falling, crumbling, God is unchanging. The desert becomes a conversion point, a place in our life where our trust shifts from ourself to our God.

Whether our wilderness results from change in relationships, health, living situation, occupation or spiritual journey, ultimately any wilderness of external change is about a deeper change. Transitions become transformation opportunities, spiritual disciplines externally imposed, when seen in the light of God's hopes for our life.

TRAVELOGUE

• *Dump onto paper your thoughts about your place in life's journey. How do you feel, what do you think, where is God in all of this?*

• *What baggage might you discard on your journey?*

• *What longings can you identify as you take stock in your wilderness?*

During this transition time, the only constant we have is this unchanging God, in whom is no shadow of turning. God guides our steps, assures us of protection and presence, and promises to cross the land with us. He is working just beyond the headlights of our life, inviting us deeper into abandoning our own shortsighted, vision-oriented, "show me then I'll trust" approach. Because in faith, in this place of conversion, God asks us into abandonment—to let go of our need to control, to see the path before starting out. Faith is not walking by sight; it is a midnight stumble on a moonless stretch of dirt.

Transition means passage from one stage or state or location to another. Passage means that in the fullness of time we pass through and arrive at a new destination. The word promises a crossing over. Though abandonment feelings are not uncommon in barren lands, we are never left to our own devices. No, we sojourn with the God who says, "See, I am doing a new thing! Now it springs up; do you not perceive it? I am making a way in the desert and streams in the wasteland" (Isaiah 43:19).

In places of seeming aloneness, it is easy to forget that God provides a way in the desert. We lose our spiritual bearings in the wastelands when we close our eyes against the blowing sand. In Isaiah 43 the Israelites failed to appreciate their trailbreaking God. Even the wild animals honored him because "'I provide water in the desert and streams in the wasteland, to give drink to my people, my chosen, the people I formed for myself that they may proclaim my praise. Yet you have not called upon me,' says the Lord" (Isaiah 43:20-22).

Wilderness experts know it is unwise to travel alone. And although the wilderness feels alone and lonely, we are never without God's guiding hand. The peril lies in believing that because we cannot see that hand, we must drag ourself through the tough times and land on the other side by our own clever and carefully honed wilderness survival skills.

The gift of the wilderness is that it is best navigated with help from God. He *wants* us to call on him.

TENDER SOULS

Think of the Israelites traversing the desert in sandals. Wasn't that broiling sand hot on bare toes? But hot or not, turning back was not a choice. Though they whined about the desert ("If only we had died by the LORD's hand in Egypt!" Exodus 16:3), to go backward meant certain death. They had to go forward and figure out what to do with their anxiety and fear on the journey; they could not wince, grimace and hotfoot it back to Egypt, with their hearts stiffened by anger, pain and resentment.

Turning back is not really a choice for us, either. Most transitions are not reversible. Even so, too often we take the return-to-Egypt approach with our spirits. We ouch and grouch and idolize the great life we had before transition set upon us like a whirling tornado. We have wimpy feet and hardened hearts from our wilderness forays. We need instead tough soles and tender souls. A desert danger is that we encase our heart in stone, steeling ourselves against the pain of change, and then lose the opportunities of meeting and being sustained by God along the way, of being changed by the journey.

The heart is a sensitive instrument. Sometimes our feelings hurt so that we prefer death: prefer not to feel, to move into anesthetized living, to concentrate on putting one foot in front of the other and just getting through. Survival is our only goal. But transition's wilderness is not really about the dilemma at hand: how bad the job or the teenager is, how much you want a baby or a husband, or don't want the one you have.

THE WILDERNESS DIRECTION

We think we are on a journey through life, physically. Life is about getting through the next minute, hour, day, week, year. And sometimes that is a valid, short-term technique in crisis. But long-term, we will lose our heart with that approach. Throughout our life, God is at work, reconfiguring, transforming, remaking us. God is all about our heart, about

TRAVELOGUE

• *When have you experienced God's guidance in the wilderness?*

• *Think about the God who doesn't change. How would it feel to put all your hope in the midst of a season of change into that changeless God?*

• *When have you chosen a return-to-Egypt travel mode? When have you felt lost, without a compass? What did you do? What about your heart right now?*

healing broken places. The heat of the desert shapes us in the Heart-smith's fire.

But this goes against our self-protective habits of guarding our heart. We think guarding our heart means "Don't let anyone hurt us," so we shut down, immobilize, lock and key our heart, like a guard at the Art Institute who denies anyone access to a prized display.

Truly, though, guarding our heart means making certain we allow ourself to feel all we are supposed to feel. We refuse to allow others to shame us or frighten us into shutting down. We guard our heart, then, by giving it room to grow, to explore—and yes, be hurt, just as mothers must allow their children freedom to grow and to be hurt. The lockdown approach destroys heartful living, and in our expedition through the wilds our heart may be the bounty we seek. Bring it back alive! The desert becomes a search and rescue attempt from God. Perhaps we are on this safari not for big game but to find our own heart. And God's.

RESPONDING TO THE WILDERNESS

Given the inevitability of change, we often feel powerless, without any choices. But we do have options in transition, decisions we can make that will transform the wilderness from barrenness to bounty. Through-out our travel together, we can discover those grace points in the wilderness. We can choose to feel our desert feelings, to focus and follow God, to find the meaning and learn to flourish in spite of the pH balance of the soil of our life. Like the Israelites, we can choose to feast, to fellowship, even to find fun in the wilderness. And wrapped in all our choices is the heart response; to remember our journeys, that God's righteousness might be revealed; to not forget where he has taken us, as difficult as that path may be; and to choose to live in freedom in the desert.

WILDERNESS BLESSING

As a skinny kid growing up in southern Indiana, I found those first barefoot summer days grueling. Shoes were excessive, like a tail on a frog, to be shed as soon as possible. But our feet had grown soft from school shoes and socks, and we cringed and limped, arms flailing for balance, over gravel driveways and blazing, tar-coated streets. Within days, though, we ran across the rocks and teetered on our haunches over the sun-baked tar to pop the bubbles. Barefoot pain prepared me for the joys of childhood play. I wouldn't have missed it for the world.

I am nearing that place where I can say, "I wouldn't have missed it for the world," about those down-spikes in my life, those places where pain was huge but God even larger. We might not choose change, especially difficult change—probably wouldn't. And yet, God so wants our heart to be whole, this wilderness trip may be just the ticket.

One friend wrote me, in the midst of a season of anguish and sorting, "As much as it feels bad at times, I would fight you for it rather than let you take it away from me. Because I have a sense that there is something good on the other side—something God wants me to have, know, learn, rest in about himself, something I dearly want."

Martin Luther said,

This life therefore is not righteousness
but growth in righteousness
not health but healing
not being but becoming. . . .
We are not yet what we shall be
but we are growing toward it.
The process is not yet finished
but it is going on.
This is not the end
but it is the road.
All does not yet gleam in glory
but all is being purified.

I love Deuteronomy 1:31, describing Israel's relationship with God in the desert, "where you experienced him carrying you along like a man carries his son. This he did everywhere you went until you came to this very place" (NET). If God can do this with 600,000 men and their wives and children, then God can be there for us, as well.

In these times of change, may God carry us as a parent carries a child. And as we remember our journey, may God grant us joy in the looking back, that we might say, "I wouldn't have missed it for the world."

Wilderness Response

ACCOMPANIMENT PSALM

In you, O LORD, I have taken refuge;
   let me never be put to shame;
   deliver me in your righteousness.
Turn your ear to me,
   come quickly to my rescue;
be my rock of refuge,
a strong fortress to save me.
Since you are my rock and my fortress,
   for the sake of your name lead and guide me. . . .

Be merciful to me, O LORD, for I am in distress;
   my eyes grow weak with sorrow,
   my soul and my body with grief.
My life is consumed by anguish
   and my years by groaning;
my strength fails because of my affliction,
   and my bones grow weak. . . .

But I trust in you, O LORD;
   I say, "You are my God."
My times are in your hands. . . .
Let your face shine on your servant;
   save me in your unfailing love. . . .

You heard my cry for mercy
   when I called to you for help.

Love the LORD, all his saints!
    The LORD preserves the faithful. . . .
Be strong and take heart,
    all you who hope in the LORD.

FROM PSALM 31

DESERT READING

"Was it because there were no graves in Egypt that you brought us to the desert to die? . . . It would have been better for us to serve the Egyptians than to die in the desert!"

    Moses answered the people, "Do not be afraid. Stand firm and you will see the deliverance the LORD will bring you today. The Egyptians you see today you will never see again. The LORD will fight for you; you need only to be still."

EXODUS 14:11-14

GUIDING SONG

Abide with Me

Abide with me; fast falls the eventide;
The darkness deepens; Lord with me abide.
When other helpers fail and comforts flee,
Help of the helpless, O abide with me.

Swift to its close ebbs out life's little day;
Earth's joys grow dim; its glories pass away;
Change and decay in all around I see;
O Thou who changest not, abide with me.

I need thy presence every passing hour.
What but thy grace can foil the tempter's power?

Who, like thyself, my guide and stay can be?
Through cloud and sunshine, Lord, abide with me.
WORDS: HENRY F. LYTE, 1847
MUSIC: W. H. MONK, 1861

REMEMBER YOUR JOURNEY

- How are you reacting, before God, right now, about the wilderness times in your life and your current transition point?

- Where is God inviting you to grow, to change, to soften?

- Can you let God carry you as a daddy carries a child? What would that look like?

- Journal a prayer of response.

Still Point

In silence we will find new energy and true unity.

The energy of God will be ours to do all things well. . . .

In the silence of the heart God speaks.

If you face God in prayer and silence, God will speak to you.

Then you will know that you are nothing.

It is only when you realize your nothingness, your emptiness,

that God can fill you with Himself.

Souls of prayer are souls of great silence. . . .

Listen in silence, because if your heart is full of other things

you cannot hear the voice of God.

But when you have listened to the voice of God

in the stillness of your heart, then your heart is filled with God. . . .

Then from the fullness of our hearts, our mouth will have to speak. . . .

I shall keep the silence of my heart with greater care,

so that in the silence of my heart I hear His words of comfort

and from the fullness of my heart I comfort Jesus

in the distressing disguise of the poor.

MOTHER TERESA

2

....

CHOOSING TO FEEL

But to each one of us grace has been given as Christ apportioned it.

EPHESIANS 4:7

$\mathcal{J}$n the intense movie *The Edge,* Anthony Hopkins plays a wealthy intellectual with no real friends and no real reason for living. When their plane crashes in the Alaskan wilderness, his companions panic. Drawing on his fount of knowledge, Hopkins calmly and rationally sets about survival, stating, "Most people lost in the wilds die of shame. They ask themselves, 'What did I do wrong? How could I have gotten myself into this?' And so they sit there and they die and don't do the one thing that would have saved their lives. Thinking."

Panic is problematic in the wilderness, obscuring survival training and common sense. Thinking, and then feeling, our way through the wilds may save us, our relationships, our sanity, our faith.

EMOTIONAL HOLDING TANKS

Our first reaction in the desert of transition may be shame, as Hopkins pointed out. What's wrong with us? How can we feel this way, be in this place?

Shame speaks of past issues, and the wilderness is often a place of unfinished business and unprocessed pain. Frequently, years of stockpiling our emotions, hiding them from others and ourself, bring us to a land of barren lostness, where we no longer know who we are or why we are numb. Unfelt feelings shackle us in emotional debtor's prison. When we discover and feel those feelings, expecting them, our freedom journey begins. A way is made in the wilderness. Abba Poeman wrote, "Vigilance, self-knowledge, and discernment: these are the guides of the soul."

God is not surprised at our emotions swooping like bats under stadium lights. We may be surprised and even ashamed of them, but God knows our heart, the things hidden in secret places. If we warehouse those feelings in the dank darkness, they will seep into our conscious life like noxious gas, poisoning us and those around us. Better to be open about our feelings during fretful and frightful times of transition—and to know that some feelings may be an accumulated buildup from years of tamping them down, ignoring them, smiling bravely and moving forward with an anesthetized heart.

The heart-numbing desert tempts us to stay numb. When feelings do not return, invite God to open your heart again, to reveal the blockage and restore feelings. Do not be afraid to name and feel those feelings. Feelings tune us into our heart and our deepest longings and then can either run our life or help us run to God. But even with a numbness of spirit, God is not bound: all will be well, someday.

FEELING, BUT NOT FINE

After a famine in Canaan forced their move to Egypt, the Israelites enjoyed MVA (Most Valuable Alien) status for hundreds of years in Egypt under the Pharaohs during their ancestor Joseph's life and legacy. But their hiatus turned into a Hades of slavery under the cruel, greedy, jealous reign of the current ruler. Threatened by their numbers, he "put slave masters over them to oppress them with forced labor" and "made their lives bitter with hard labor in mortar and bricks and with all kinds of work in the fields; in all their hard labor the Egyptians used them ruthlessly" (Exodus 1:11, 14).

After centuries of bondage, the entire Jewish nation protested this injustice to God. They were not mum about their feelings. "The Israelites groaned in their slavery and cried out, and their cry for help because of their slavery went up to God" (Exodus 2:23).

Hear the Israelites' feelings? They groaned, cried out; their cry was desperate. "The word for this painfully intense 'groaning' appears elsewhere to describe a response to having two broken arms (Ezekiel 30:24)." This was no subtle moaning, no retiring to one's bed to weep silently, no stuffing of emotions. They "cried out," meaning, "shriek from anguish or danger." This was corporate shrieking and shouting before God.

TRAVELOGUE

• *What emotions have you stored, what events have you ignored, for fear of others' reactions or even of your own reaction? Why? How has this helped or hindered your traveling?*

• *Consider God's promise of deliverance. What happens within as you contemplate that pledge (Exodus 2:23-24)? Do you feel angry that he seems slow in following through? Can you give yourself permission to "shriek from anguish or danger" with God?*

God's response moves me. "And God heard their groaning, and God remembered his covenant with Abraham, with Isaac, and with Jacob. God saw the Israelites and God had compassion" (Exodus 2:24-25 NET). The word for *hear* means "responding to what is heard"; sometimes it even means "to obey." God didn't passively listen; *remember* means "to begin to act on the basis of what is being remembered." The Israelites' feelings tapped into God's heart. He heard and honored their feelings; he felt compassion (literally, "to suffer with") for them. He sprang into action. In fact, he had already chosen the deliverer: Moses.

God hadn't forgotten his covenant with Abraham and his family; the time simply hadn't come to fulfill it. Nor has God forgotten us in our private wilderness of change. God's timing has much to do with the readiness and receptivity of our heart, our willingness to acknowledge our anguish and cry out—shriek—before God, to relinquish our self-mastery and turn our heart and future over to him. Our helplessness and humility may be the soul cry for which God waits. He hears, has compassion and will deliver. At just the right time.

His promise still holds.

THE LANGUAGE OF THE WILDERNESS

Search and rescue teams watch for signals from people stranded in perilous places. Whether a fire, a flag or sticks forming particular shapes, desert language includes specific ground-to-air signals to indicate the survivor's status: OK, wounded, help. So we need to embrace the language of transition: our feelings.

Wilderness terrain is no place for pretense, for stuffing down feelings and slogging forward courageously. When Rich and I began this missionary type of employment, when fear, anger and panic regularly gripped me, my friend Linda said, "Keep sharing your feelings with your husband during this time." Honesty prevents walls of misunderstanding and anger from growing, and it keeps us from barring loved ones from our heart.

If the wilderness involves pain inflicted by another, David Viscott, M.D., says, "The secret of mental health [is] to tell the person who hurt you that they hurt you, when they hurt you." This prohibits toxic internal buildup. We can do this tactfully, without ugliness or blame, at the right time, but we must learn this part of desert language. Otherwise, the internal heat of the wilderness creates combustion, compounding the misery.

People process life events and circumstances in different ways. We may view feelings as inaccurate if they do not rationally align with those facts. Men may well focus on the play-by-play details; women may tune in to the overall tone and feeling of a relationship or situation. But feelings go beyond facts and are God's means of getting our attention; we can't rationalize them away or say they aren't true.

Along our journey through the barrens, we must know what to expect. Don't be alarmed if you feel like King David: "My bed swims because of my tears." You aren't springing leaks—your body is trying to tell you something.

TRANSITION'S TEARS

Tears are part of our wilderness language. After I spoke to a seminary group about transitions, telling them to expect tears and feel free to weep, women poured toward me to talk. "I didn't know it was OK to cry." "I try not to feel this, but the tears still come."

These women were training for kingdom service, either as clergy spouses or in other ministries. These women, who would be called on to hold the weeping forms of others, did not know that tears were part of their own personal package. Tears are vital ingredients in wilderness survival; just as they physically cleanse our eyes of impurities, they also release our feelings. Someone has said that if we do not cry, holding back our tears will cause other organs to weep. The pain will find an exit route, one way or the other.

Lois's life was like the stock car races, one accident or problem after another. She said, "I can't let down and cry or I'll fall apart." Could her dangerously elevated blood pressure be related to holding back tears?

With crying, God cleanses us of distress, contamination, anger. Tears honor this time in our life and the value of those over whom we weep. Crying as a tool leads us out of our helplessness and even self-pity into Christ's sufficiency. Tears symbolize our humanity, demonstrate our capacity to feel deeply and, when we get past any self-pity that may open the

TRAVELOGUE

• *How do you store*

your feelings? When do they pop

up? What happens when you

verbalize them to God, to

yourself and to others?

• *In what times of your life have*

you found tears to be your

constant companion? Or when

have you choked back tears,

clogging your emotional tear

ducts in the process? What has

this done to you?

• *Where, now, do you feel the press*

of tears? Can you wait with them

before God?

spigot, empty us of ourself. They become a gift, a sacrifice, a fellowship offering to God.

Ken Gire affirms in *Windows of the Soul*, "The closest communion with God comes, I believe, through the sacrament of tears. Just as grapes are crushed to make wine and grain to make bread, so the elements of this sacrament come from the crushing experiences of life." We cry through our prayers and pray through our tears, and God waters the desert soil of our heart.

DESERT FATIGUE

Nancy turned off her engine in the parking lot. *I'll close my eyes a minute, then run in and get groceries,* she thought. She awakened an hour later, startled, shaking from exhaustion. Transition was her middle name. With an unemployed husband and boomerang children, she also ran her own business and cared for a sister who had cancer. She volunteered endlessly at church. Though any single such transition would take its toll, she couldn't understand her relentless fatigue.

There is no tired like Transition Tired. We should expect battle fatigue from living in the wilderness and accommodate it. Instead, we live as if sleeping were dangerous—or weak. What would it look like to rest in the wilderness?

We need to wait out the heat of the deserts—our routines may need overhauling or adjustment, adding rest to our desert regimen. Shirley's fifteen-minute power nap rejuvenates her flagging energy. I try to eliminate late-night work and rarely attempt to outlast my teenagers. Gena, in a yearlong recovery from burnout and illness, says, "I refuse to live on adrenaline any longer. When I am tired, I rest." Some people exercise to lessen fatigue since exercise re-creates energy. (This has multiple benefits: it reduces stress, strengthens the heart and helps us to live longer. Any day now I will try this approach. Right now I am . . . too tired.)

Deep, quiet prayer before God brings rest unlike any other discipline. In silence, when we offer God our baggage—the anxious longings and fears and tears and all other heart-weights—we transfer the burden to the One who intended all along to bear it. "Come to Me, all who are weary and heavy-laden, and I will give you rest. Take My yoke upon you, and learn from Me, for I am gentle and humble in heart, and you will find rest for your souls. For My yoke is easy, and My burden is light" (Matthew 11:28-30 NASB).

TOUCHY TRAVELERS

During wilderness travel, we can be as prickly as the cacti and feel as void as the landscape. When reactions come first and feelings second, don't be shocked. Expect to be tender, touchy, reactionary; your emotions may be closer to the surface than normal. A tiny irritant, like a splinter under a fingernail, makes the whole fingertip swell and throb. Transition is no tiny irritant, and out-of-proportion reactions are not uncommon.

Neither are controlling and micromanagement. Powerless to effect change over the changes affecting us, we attempt to control all the details for the people around us. We may explode over little things because the big picture far outreaches our manipulative abilities. Aware of this natural tendency, we can begin to let God loosen our tight fists.

Too, we veer between desert extremes in transitions. We may experience polarity of emotions, just like the cold nights sometimes follow sweltering days. I find myself near tears and longing for comfort, then fighting off closeness because of the emotional energy being close necessitates.

DESERT GRIEF

Grief seems obvious if the transition is the death of a loved one. But grief is also a broader place of regret, whether for times lost, loved ones gone, broken dreams or wrong turns. One woman never grieved her dad's unavailability. A thirty-year-old buried her grief over her promiscuity. Another never stopped to mourn her miscarriages. The wish-I-had-dones rise and clog our heart; the wish-I-hadn't-dones incapacitate us until we let them out, pray them out and cry them out before God. We may not even know we're grieving until it surfaces in surprising ways: controlling, or anger, or exhaustion, or regret, or shame or depression. Perhaps it assumes the guise of busyness or other addictive behavior. Not feeling the grief, disowning our loss, throttles the spirit and chokes our growth.

Anne Lamott writes:

> The lifelong fear of grief keeps us in a barren, isolated place and . . . only grieving can heal grief. . . . [I]t is at once intolerable and a great opportunity. . . . It is only by experiencing that ocean of sadness in a naked and immediate way that we come to be healed— which is to say, that we come to experience life with a real sense of presence and spaciousness and peace.

Our work in the wilderness includes grieving. Grieving eventually gives way to healing, acceptance and the ability to thrive again.

ADMITTING ANGER

The death of Millie's parents left behind years scarred by unforgiveness and blame. They had attacked her after her sister's death, asking, "Why couldn't it have been you?" She never felt good enough, special or loved.

Admitting anger and pain over her past helped clarify some of the life compromises she had made: health issues, her unforgiveness of those who had hurt her, a fear of abandonment. Only honest anger could pull her to the only One capable of carrying that pain, the One who felt it every bit as much as she.

Perhaps we are angry at God. *How can he let this happen? How can he abandon me like this? Where is he when I need him? I've lived a good life— and what do I get for it?* God knows our heart, knows our anger at him and waits for us to talk about it.

Anger is an ordinary reaction to life in an unjust world, filled with imperfect people, polluted with mixed messages and hidden agendas. Moses and the Israelites were angry—at one another and at God. God is OK with that anger. Properly directed, anger can be a clarifying agent, freeing us to examine our soul, pray out our pain and misery, and short-circuit depression, which is buried anger.

FACING FEAR

Fear is natural, especially when we reside in the unknown. In most times of transition, the unknown looms large, the primary variable in the formula for the future.

A friend sent this word to me in one of my many bouts of survival-of-the-self-employed fear: "You are loved in your tears. It is OK for anger to lick up and fear to fly around. It's OK to scream. God is always only after something that includes your own good."

Permission to feel fear is vital. Faith doesn't mean the absence of fear, but the mind and heart moving forward into an unknown or unlikely situation in spite of fear. Both anger and fear can draw us to God, who alone knows the plans he has in store for us and has our welfare at the core. In the swirling chasm of the unknown, it helps to remember truth: that God is good, that our future is held securely in those strong hands, that every event of our life is intended to tow us more deeply toward dependency on God.

TELLING THE TRUTH

One transition task is to let others know what to expect. Realistically, can they rely on our superhuman performances as in days past? What is honest during your "grace period"? If you need to relinquish or downgrade places of responsibility, whether they be a spotless home or nursery duty at church, frame the words to communicate that. If your tears are frequent and your smiles few, let loved ones in on the pain. They need to understand the source of your tears, know that God is working on your heart and that this time of pain will result in transformation in due time.

God's heart bends toward the wanderer, the exile, the homeless—toward *us* as we roam this wilderness. This is clear from Old Testament laws: "Do not oppress an alien; you yourselves know how it feels to be aliens, because you were aliens in Egypt" (Exodus 23:9). Our experience in time of exile and alienation will change the way we treat others. As we embrace transition's symptoms in ourself, we will see them in others and our heart too will bend toward the wanderer.

TRAVELOGUE

• *What's your fatigue level right now? How do you sense your tiredness compromising your journey? What would keep you from resting?*

• *When does grief grip you? anger, fear? How can you let those feelings lead you to God?*

LOOKING FOR JOY

As I prepared dinner one night, the worst terrors of the self-employed attacked. My mind reeled like an out-of-control movie camera—*we'll have to sell the house and all our possessions, pull the kids out of school, our teeth will fall out without dental care, we'll move two thousand miles away where the cost of living is cheaper—*scrub, chop, sauté, all the while feeling this soul inflammation.

TRAVELOGUE

• *What expectations and needs must you communicate with others during this time?*

• *When have you found joy in the place of pain? How do you feel about that?*

Without bidding, a passage from Scripture I memorized twenty years ago formed words in my brain:

> Consider it all joy . . . when you encounter various trials, knowing that the testing of your faith produces endurance. And let endurance have its perfect result, that you may be perfect and complete, lacking in nothing. But if any of you lacks wisdom, let [that person] ask of God, who gives to all [people] generously and without reproach, and it will be given. (James 1:2-5 NASB)

Joy is not a feeling I expect in places of pain. Certainly it is not the reaction I tend to display over various trials. The original word for joy expresses abundance: full joy, greatest joy, all joy. Interesting that our greatest joy is to be in the result of our testing, the transformation that comes from the trials. But only when we do our heartwork—feeling our feelings, owning them and being honest with others about them, allowing them to lead us to, rather than separate us from, God—only when we are faithful about our heart can transition be a means of transformation.

Our grace point, our intersection with God's divine enabling, becomes the ability to feel. Even in the wilderness.

Wilderness Response

ACCOMPANIMENT PSALM

Be merciful to me, LORD, for I am faint;
  O LORD, heal me, for my bones are in agony.
My soul is in anguish.
  How long, O LORD, how long?

Turn, O LORD, and deliver me;
Save me because of your unfailing love. . . .

I am worn out from groaning;
  all night long I flood my bed with weeping
  and drench my couch with tears.
My eyes grow weak with sorrow;
  they fail me because of all my foes. . . .

  The LORD has heard my weeping.
The LORD has heard my cry for mercy;
  the LORD accepts my prayer.

PSALM 6:2-4, 6-9

DESERT READING

I will sing to the LORD,
  for he is highly exalted.
The horse and its rider
  he has hurled into the sea.
The LORD is my strength and my song;
  he has become my salvation.
He is my God, and I will praise him,
  my father's God, and I will exalt him.
The LORD is a warrior;
  the LORD is his name. . . .

In your unfailing love you will lead
   the people you have redeemed.
In your strength you will guide them
   to your holy dwelling. . . .
You will bring them in and plant them
   on the mountain of your inheritance—
the place, O LORD, you made for your dwelling,
   the sanctuary, O LORD, your hands established.
The LORD will reign for ever and ever.
EXODUS 15:1-3, 13, 17-18

GUIDING SONG

Give to the Winds Thy Fears
(sung to the tune of "Rise Up, O Men of God")

Give to the winds thy fears;
hope and be undismayed.
God hears thy sighs and counts thy tears,
God shall lift up thy head.

Through waves and clouds and storms,
God gently clears thy way;
Wait thou God's time;
so shall this night soon end in joyous day.
WORDS: PAUL GERHARDT, 1653;
TRANSLATED BY JOHN WESLEY, 1739
MUSIC: WILLIAM H. WALTER, 1894

REMEMBER YOUR JOURNEY

- Pour out your feelings before God. Don't try to edit them. Then pray your tears, letting them wet God's shoulder.

Still Point

Come, in my labor find a resting place

And in my sorrows lay your head,

Or rather take my life and blood

And buy yourself a better bed—

Or take my breath and take my death

And buy yourself a better rest.

THOMAS MERTON

3
....

CHOOSING TO FOLLOW

And God is able to make all grace abound to you, that always having

all sufficiency in everything, you may have an abundance for every good deed.

2 CORINTHIANS 9:8 NASB

How do we follow God in a place of darkness, when no light shines in front of us, only the underbelly of storm clouds of the spirit? How do we follow with neither pillar of fire nor tower of smoke advising us? When we've lost our bearings and no one shouts marching orders and life has blindsided us? When we're waiting for test results or a spouse to return or a prodigal child to turn around? When the transition point is a broken relationship or the death of a child or sudden unemployment or deteriorating health?

How do we follow when we are too tired to move, to think? When so many obstacles surround us that we are checkmated? How do we follow when it feels as though we're the last soldier defending the Alamo?

How do we find east, if the sun never rises and the moon and stars cannot guide us and the compass of our soul is broken? Traditional signs—moss on the north side of buildings and rocks and trees—don't necessarily work in the wilderness, and traditional means of following God may differ in the desert.

44 G R A C E   P O I N T S

FOLLOW THE LEADER

For the Israelites, the wilderness was a refuge, a safe place, a point of deliverance by the almighty God Yahweh from the cruel hands and demands of Pharaoh. Rather than a place of devastation, the desert became
a place of follow-ship, where the people learned to follow the Lord—
where they found again and again that God's hand was for them, to save
and not to harm, to deliver and provide a good land full of fruit and blessing. Moses had to learn to follow God and had to make it clear to Pharaoh
and to his own kinfolk that the Israelites were following God as well.

The enemy's tactic is to detract supporters in the wilderness, to get
people to renounce their followership. Moses innately knew this and
questioned the Lord: "What if they don't follow me? What'll I tell them?
What if they don't believe me?" (Exodus 3:11; 4:1, 10 paraphrased). The
answer for Moses resounded clearly: "I will be with you. . . . I AM WHO I
AM" (Exodus 3:12, 14). Following implies that a leader is willing to reveal himself, longing to lead, worthy of our trust. Following isn't about
us, our abilities or spiritual techniques, our convincing or conniving; it
is about the One we follow.

The Israelites learned at tremendous cost that following their own
way and their own wisdom meant losing. When Moses climbed up the
mountain to receive the Ten Commandments, the people quickly in-
vented and followed their own ideas about faithfulness. Witness the
golden calf scene at the foot of Mount Sinai, when the Hebrews grew
weary of waiting for Moses to return and melted their own god out of
hand-me-down jewelry (Exodus 32). While we may not see God, while
we may be exhausted waiting for him, we can't lose sight of his heart and
desires for us, nor let go of his hand.

And in the desert, faith does not always look sensible. (Would all those
women who accompanied the 600,000 men have packed up their homes
and children if they'd expected forty years of tent camping in the desert?!)

Deuteronomy 1 recounts the Israelites' arrival at the edge of the Promised Land. Moses reminded them of God's faithfulness through their

desert flight, and then he urged them into the next stage of the adventure, the reason for fleeing Egypt, the promise they had clung to for forty dry and dusty days. By now, they should have been experts at "Follow the Leader." But like me, they wanted to reinvent the rules. How boring, always obeying, never leading, never having creative, stunning moments of authority. So when Moses said, "See, the LORD your God has given you the land. Go up and take possession of it as the LORD, the God of your fathers, told you. Do not be afraid; do not be discouraged" (Deuteronomy 1:21), the Israelites had a bright idea.

"Let us send men ahead to spy out the land for us and bring back a report about the route we are to take and the towns we will come to" (Deuteronomy 1:22). Some (but not all) of the spies brought back an ominous accounting of unconquerable giants in the land—and the people refused to follow God. Why, after all the tromping and trudging and ultimately trusting, did they need scouts to tell them how to proceed? With God leading, they had the ultimate Eye in the Sky: they never had to worry about the route, never had to deploy scouts to check out stops.

But we are the same. With God leading, we too need never worry. Yet, even with years of God's faithfulness filling our spiritual banks, we decide we can only trust what our eyes can see, what our limited vision portrays. The enemies assume monstrous proportions, and our heart quells with fear. We go it alone, weigh the odds, calculate and strategize. Proverbs calls it being wise in our own eyes and warns us against it.

There are better strategies for learning to follow.

FOLLOW GOD BY CLINGING

Fresh out of college and on the road to independence, I found myself driving everywhere. My new love affair with God frequently uppermost in my mind and heart, I prayed out loud while driving. But, adding years, marriage, children, distraction, fatigue, endless lists and crowding anxiety, that intimate pray-aloud time flew out the window. The years have rolled past faster than I can roll up the car window, it seems, and driving has become just a means to an end, not a connecting point with God.

Last week, on the road again, I began to deliberately "set my mind on Christ" even though worries sidetracked me like roadside debris flapping in the air. I started "taking every thought captive" by praying out loud again. I prayed not with a list of needs and problems for God to handle but with a thankful heart for God's attributes. For who he is.

Holiness came up. And loving-kindness. And omnipotence. Knowing that absolute power corrupts absolutely, God's all-powerfulness could concern me. But the complete picture of our Triune God is one in which each characteristic balances the others. God's holiness prohibits him from acting unjustly or with favoritism in our life. God's love prevents him from meting out justice alone without grace. With our Lord there are unbreakable checks and balances.

Warmth flowed over me as I realized that, although I cannot envision the future from this place, obscured by flowing desert sands and mountains too vast to conquer, I can trust the God who loves me, controls the world, acts justly with grace, forgives totally. Even though few people make it freelance in the world of writing and music, our future, our every breath, is secure in the hands of this God.

Knowing this makes following God easier, for wherever God leads, the results will be good. Not necessarily predictable, but good. So I cling, not to the unknown future or to the been-there, done-that past, but to the God I know, to the faithful, just, loving, holy God who claims me as his child and will always tote me in the right direction, like a baby propped on a strong arm and bobbling along for the ride.

"When I remember You on my bed, I meditate on You in the night watches, for You have been my help, and in the shadow of Your wings I sing for joy. My soul clings to You; Your right hand upholds me," the psalmist sings (Psalm 63:6-8 NASB). Clinging makes sense. Clinging will save our life and bring us home.

FOLLOW GOD BY FOLLOWING OTHERS' TRACKS

There are a few people in my life who, if they said, "Come with me, I want you to accompany me on a trip," I would follow them anywhere— except through foaming wild whitewater or perhaps a snake-filled river in a tropical climate. Because I have tracked their lives and their spiritual trails for years, I know that they have clung to God. They have out-sat the darkness, waiting for the light to appear. They have put in time in their own personal Alamos. They have learned to listen to the God of the desert, the God of the still small voice, and they help *me* hear, as well. With my world a whirlwind, others' stories bend my ear and teach me.

The desert becomes an earphone where others' journeys inform our own. We might hear of another's soul travels through books or articles. But I also listen to conversations around me, trying to learn from the women and men who are triumphing in the face of trauma and transition. One woman's tactic for getting through sleepless nights: "Pray the Lord's Prayer, over and over." We can listen and be encouraged by others' sojourns, and we can learn to trust God's voice spoken through mentors along the way.

Trust is essential to following. Our society is based on trust: trusting that drivers won't hit us, that cashiers will count our change correctly, that taxis will take the fastest route, that the elevator will stop at the right floor, and that the food we buy and the medications we use are safe. We trust that teachers will care for our children; pastors, our soul; doctors, our body. All of whom are fallible.

Can we trust the God who is infallible but hidden from our sight?

TRAVELOGUE

• *Share your struggle to follow at this time in your life. What does it feel like, what is your heart saying, what do your tears tell you?*

• *What can you cling to about God? What don't you trust about God?*

After a meeting in Chicago, my husband put on his in-line skates and headed for the path along Lake Michigan. Insane, life-defying traffic whizzed around him. From behind, a young man called out, "Can I follow you?" Rich turned around to see a blind skater with a white-tipped cane rolling toward him. Trustingly falling into line behind Rich, the blind man's cane swept the pavement between him and my husband's skates. What an image of God leading us. Though we are without vision for the future, though it feels perilous, he will not let our skates turn in the wrong direction if we follow the tracks he lays down for us.

FOLLOW GOD BY STAYING TRUE

Two weeks after we said yes to God's call out of the local pastorate and into this itinerate sort of ministry, I tallied my share of financial responsibility. How was I to follow when needing to earn five times beyond my current income? The figure seemed insurmountable. Other options further discouraged me. My mind jumped frantically, like kids and marbles bouncing on a trampoline. Should I apply for a job at the bank? cashier? substitute teach? What about this sense of calling? What about my family?

Honking geese awakened me early one weekend at a retreat center where I was speaking, a hundred trumpets warming up outside the window. My head immediately filled with worry, the intake anxiety valve stuck on open. My heart felt like the Titanic, with water from the Atlantic Ocean pouring through every crevice and crack.

Outside, the geese quieted. One hunkered down under a tree twenty feet away, its oblong body stationary, webbed feet hidden beneath thick down. The neck, however, like a vacuum cleaner hose, swiveled everywhere. The goose rubbed its cheek on its back! It was sitting, but not still, fretting with feathers, nipping, chewing, rubbernecking.

What a picture of my heart. I too was sitting, but not still. My fretting was like attempting self-direction in a sandstorm. Chastened, I blurted the worries to God. Opened the Scriptures. The day's reading included Joshua 1:7-8 (NASB): "Do not turn . . . to the right or to the left. . . . Then you will make your way prosperous, and then you will have success."

Is turning to the left or right like getting a job out of line with my passions and calling? After all, God had called me to write and speak. Was that straight ahead? God's whisper through Joshua was to follow by staying true to the longings in my heart. God would provide; God could define and be responsible for "success."

Home again, the phone rang.

TRAVELOGUE

• *Remember times of lostness in the past. When did you experience God's faithfulness?*

• *What dreams stir your heart? Are you tempted to abandon them in the wilderness?*

A Texas voice said, "We met last year; might I refer you for speaking engagements that I cannot take?" Her referral prompted a phone call from Mexico to lead a retreat. I was stewing about getting to the next suburb to minister, and God was planning a trip to a mountainside resort.

If we believe the Scriptures, if we believe the Lord's promises to give us the desires of our heart, if we only will delight in him (Psalm 37:3-4), if we believe that "the LORD longs to be gracious" to us (Isaiah 30:18 NASB), then we must out of obedience stay true to the dreams planted in our heart by the Lord of the harvest. Dreams make sense, especially in transition times, only when gripping tightly the hand of the God of the impossible.

FOLLOWING GOD BY HEART

Some days, though, I just don't want to hang on. I don't want to cling. I just want off the boat. I want to wallow. I have no energy to dredge up, no backbone to stiffen, no shoulders to square.

At this point, our journey is not about our feelings—although we must learn to recognize them and respect them and let those feelings lead us to God—our journey is about moving in the right direction. If we do the next right thing, the heart will follow. However, our life with Christ must not be an act, an outward show without inward heart compliance and change. This is not "making nice" with our insides shattering. If, after doing the next right thing, the heart does not follow, then it is time to sit still, to eliminate clutter from life and mind and heart through repentance, prayer, accountability and rest.

God wants the very best for each of us, and we cannot always see this with our dim, dust-rimmed eyes. Transitions are not about solving our problems: taking care of the overwhelming bills, or the reprobate child, or the disenfranchised family member, or getting a different or a better-paying or a closer job. They are about becoming who God dreams us to be. And when our heart just isn't in it (but God is), then we move forward anyway, knowing our lines by memory and trusting God with our heart.

FOLLOWING JESUS

Why would the disciples follow a homeless, unemployed, destitute young man, leaving their nets and jobs and possessions and families? They left everything—talk about transitions!—to follow this man. What was it—is it—about Jesus to which they responded, we respond? Does their willingness to follow Jesus, who at this point hadn't raised the dead or fed the hungry or healed the lame, does it have anything to do with the fact that Jesus was just in from his own wilderness experience?

TRAVELOGUE

• *What have you seen*

in Christ that entices you, that

will allow you to follow?

Luke 4:1-14 recounts the propelling of Christ into the wilderness. For Jesus the desert marked our Savior's transition into the fullness of his calling and was both testing and trusting, preparation and perseverance. But here's the beauty of the wilderness: the Scriptures tell us that "Jesus, full of the Holy Spirit, . . . was led around by the Spirit in the wilderness" (Luke 4:1 NASB). This was not a willy-nilly trip where Satan dragged a powerless Jesus around in the sand. No, the Holy Spirit led, protected and guarded him, and he returned from the wilderness to Galilee "in the power of the Spirit."

Somehow, the disciples saw in Christ someone who knew where he was going—heaven, perhaps?—and they fixed their eyes on him and on the future he promised, with no earthly idea that it would involve a desert, a cross. *Multiple* crosses, as they learned to die to themselves and live in Christ's power. Tabernacling—tent camping—in the wilderness isn't appealing at all, unless the One who tabernacles with us is the Christ, and unless he himself becomes our tabernacle, our home and refuge, our bivouac, our safe place (John 1:14 NASB, marginal reading). Why follow Jesus into the wilderness? Because he promises both fruit and fulfillment. "Come, follow me . . . and I will make you fishers of men" (Matthew 4:19).

THE GOD OF THE WILDERNESS

At a conference, I spent hours counseling women individually, praying with and for them, speaking in main sessions. Many desert experiences filled that room. These women knew the grain and grit of transitions. God reminded us about owning "the cattle on a thousand hills" (Psalm 50:10 NASB). When our wilderness feels destitute, financially perilous, knowing that God owns all that livestock and can certainly take care of our needs, brings comfort.

But even in remembering the frightening, precarious, faith-wracking terrain we cross in this desert sojourn—whether finances or family, health or hearth, car or career—the God who owns all the cattle in this vast world, this God also owns all the sand dunes, the cacti, the barren straits, the wind.

This God is the God of the desert as well. The Lord of the wilderness. This God we can follow to the ends of the earth. Because the wilderness with Jesus is better than the plush, lush landscapes without him. Because we know how the story ends when the God of the wilderness holds our hand.

FOLLOW ME

Our youngest child, at age eleven, came home from an audition for a musical. "Want me to show you the routine I learned?" he asked. Rich and I watched his twenty-second dance. Then Josh said, "Mom, do you know how to waltz?" I grinned, shook my head. My dance steps are pretty rusty. "Come on, Mom. Get up. I'll show you." He pulled me to my feet. "Put your hand out here. Like this. Your other hand here. Yes." He looked me in the eye, mine only a few inches higher than his. "Now. Follow me."

I did. I looked at his sweet face, so much more grown up than last week. I barely refrained from blubbering at him and his dearness as he one-two-three'd me around the room. And we waltzed.

Even in the wilderness, following becomes a dance of trust. Choosing to follow becomes a grace point in the desert. Imagine Jesus being led through the wilderness by the Holy Spirit. Imagine him leading you now. Watch his eyes and put your right hand in his, your left hand on his shoulder. He will lead. Now follow him. And dance.

Wilderness Response

ACCOMPANIMENT PSALM

Show me your ways, O LORD,
teach me your paths;
guide me in your truth and teach me,
for you are God my Savior,
and my hope is in you all day long.
Remember, O LORD, your great mercy and love,
for they are from of old.
Remember not the sins of my youth
and my rebellious ways;
according to your love remember me,
for you are good, O LORD.

Good and upright is the LORD;
therefore he instructs sinners in his ways.
He guides the humble in what is right
and teaches them his way.

PSALM 25:4-9

DESERT READING

See, I am sending an angel ahead of you to guard you along the
way and to bring you to the place I have prepared.

EXODUS 23:20

In a desert land he found him,
in a barren and howling waste.
He shielded him and cared for him;
he guarded him as the apple of his eye,

like an eagle that stirs up its nest
  and hovers over its young,
that spreads its wings to catch them
  and carries them on its pinions.
The LORD alone led him.
DEUTERONOMY 32:10-12

GUIDING SONG

Take Thou My Hands and Lead Me

Take Thou my hands and lead me along life's way,
Until earth's night is banished by radiant day.
I would not take a single step apart from Thee;
Where Thou dost walk or tarry, there let me be.

Within Thy grace so tender I would abide.
Thy perfect peace my portion whate'er betide.
I kneel dear Lord, before Thee believingly.
Thy helpless child would trust though I cannot see.

I may not glimpse Thy footprints, nor feel Thy pow'r,
Yet Thou dost draw me goalward tho' dark the hour.
Then, take my hands and lead me, thro' storm-swept night,
Till earth's devious ways have ended. In heaven's pure delight.
WORDS: JULIA HAUSMANN

REMEMBER YOUR JOURNEY

- Name the places of barren wilderness in your life. Can you offer them in prayer to the God of the desert?

Still Point

In retrospect I can see in my own life

what I could not see at the time—

how the job I lost helped me find work I needed to do,

how the "road closed" sign turned me toward terrain I needed to travel,

how losses that felt irredeemable forced me to

discern meanings I needed to know.

On the surface, it seemed that life was lessening,

but silently and lavishly the seeds of new life

were always being sown.

PARKER J. PALMER

4

....

CHOOSING TO FIND THE MEANING

Each one should use whatever gift . . . received to serve others,

faithfully administering God's grace in its various forms.

1 PETER 4:10

$\mathcal{M}$arianne breezed in from church with her two small children, shouting a "hey" to her husband working in the basement.

The next thing she remembers is an explosion. She flew through the window onto the patio below. A neighbor, hearing the blast, found her and pulled her to safety.

The house burned to the ground, taking in its inferno the lives of her husband and boys. "I lost everything that day except my very life. My family. My home. I didn't even have a photo of my husband or children." She also lost both legs. Lying in the hospital bed, being fitted for prosthetics, learning to walk again, she vowed, "I will get well, and I will figure out why this happened to me."

Now, twenty-five years later, Marianne is on the board of the Amputee Coalition of America. She says, "I still don't know why. I asked questions: What did I do to deserve this? But it wasn't my fault—bad things happen." She shrugs and grins. We admire her shoes on her artificial feet. "But the years have allowed me to help a lot of people."

WHY IS RIGHT

"Why did this happen to me?" is a question we don't always get answered. But it is fair to ask if we want to maximize the value of our time
in the desert, because God is a God of redemption and will not allow our
pain to be wasted. With the dust of the desert clinging to our pores, we
redeem our wilderness by choosing to find meaning in the travail.

So we ask, "How can I turn to God in this place of pain, or loss, or
seeming injustice, or anger? What can I learn of God here? What do I
know of him? How might he be working through this situation? What
does God want to do with me now? What do I learn about myself here?"
Whatever our age or life stage, we ask the questions without self-pity or
whining, but honestly seeking God's heart in our wilderness rather than
withdrawing and turning inward.

One of the names for God is Jehovah-Rapha, meaning "the God who
heals" (Exodus 15:26). Asking these questions too soon can short-circuit
the healing and internal growth our Rapha-God wants to do in our life;
we must do the heart work of feeling, following and focusing to arrive at
the place of asking these questions.

So often we query everyone but the One who most cares for us: first
we need to bring our questions to God. The Lord says, "They do not cry
out to me from their hearts but wail upon their beds. . . . They do not
turn to the Most High" (Hosea 7:14, 16).

SOUL-SHIFTS AND SLOWING

Willingness to process and seek growth through the desert watches requires reflection. But it's hard to reflect in the middle of a marathon, so
a soul-slowing helps discern meaning. I would guess a caravan of around
two million people, all their livestock and wagonloads of possessions
would move slightly faster than a glacier. This is a good pace for process-
ing the journey.

When the Israelites had lived in the Land of Promise for a while (i.e., years), they were deported. Jeremiah 29:10-14 recounts the story and God's instructions: settle down, plant gardens, marry, and pray for the peace and prosperity of the city of banishment. Not only is this process considerably slower than we might desire, we might also not think of making our home in exile and settling into our present situation. Yet these are good prayer guidelines for our time of exile.

"Looking back," said my friend Steve, "helps define how we move forward." Don't they say that about history? History unexamined is destined to repeat itself? Still, we can't afford to be narcissistic voyeurs of our inner selves. We don't process just to look back—transition means passage, and that means movement. It is too tempting to get mired in the mud we create with our weeping and wailing (and whining, if you don't mind another w-word here), prohibiting us from moving on. Like those scenic overlooks on mountain drives, only from that vantage point can we see where we have been and begin to perceive the benefits blossoming from pain and problems.

Like the Israelites, we too are invited to revamp our vision for ourself and our future. Craig Barnes says, "Jesus will not settle for our watered-down dreams that accept life the way it is. He keeps pushing us toward a promise we cannot yet see."

FINDING GOD'S HEART

The wilderness process requires more than applying our mind to the problem at hand. To find meaning in our wilderness journey means we must sink our taproots deeply into our Daddy's good heart. This part of our crossing, of our desert tarrying, is also based in trust—choosing to trust God's ability to bring good out of our problems.

Remember the question to Jesus, "Rabbi, who sinned, this man or his parents, that he was born blind?" Christ answers, "[He was born blind] so that the work of God might be displayed in his life" (John 9:1-3). And then Christ healed the man. So we trust and pray that somehow, in our transition travail, God's power and work show up in our life, and with

these, vision. Trust becomes paramount to a "successful"—a transforming—desert experience. We trust, in the sweeping changes about us, that
God has good at heart and good in store.

"Fortunate are the poor in spirit," read a clip in our church bulletin
one Sunday.

> "That means: Fortunate are those who are willing
> to let themselves be censured by the word of God,
> to re-examine their views,
> to believe they haven't yet understood a thing,
> to be taken by surprise,
> to have their mind changed,
> to see their convictions,
> their principles,
> their tidy systems
> and everything they took for granted
> swept out from under them,
> and to face the fact, once for all,
> that there's no such thing as a matter of course
> and that God can ask anything." (Louis Evely)

And in our transitions, God may do just that.

A Heart for Healing

Christopher Reeve said, "It's what you do *after* a disaster that gives it
meaning." Miriam and George were only three years into their late-in-life
second marriage, falling more in love daily. The doctor's diagnosis of a
tumor on George's brain stunned them. Over the next eighteen months,
treatment, surgery and debilitation defined their days. Questions dark-
ened their nights. After her husband's death, Miriam's grief never allowed
bitterness to seep in, and eventually she found herself praying, "Lord,
you *must* have something good to bring out of this tragedy. I will trust
your timing for revealing it to me."

Her openness to God's deeper purposes created more room for healing. Before long, she journaled while on a vacation with her grown daughters: "Sometimes we need a place to be apart. . . . A place to think, to question, to re-center, to explore ourselves—past and present. Or to expand and begin, or do, that which has been calling, and has been pushed aside." A wave of realization followed: "Not a place for *me*—a place for *others* who need it."

That day, from the rich soil of sorrow, began Wellspring, Miriam's "Second Home Ministry" to crisis caregivers and a tribute to George's work with and concern for families. In its first year, over two hundred visitors found respite and grace in the sanctuary of Wellspring—and so redeemed the loss of a mighty man of God.

TRAVELOGUE

• *What questions have you asked in your wildernesses? And where have you found answers? How long did it take you to ask God rather than others?*

• *When has something good, profound, meaningful come from your pain? How did you come to the point where you saw the gift? How long between pain and meaning did you wait?*

Surely this is glory. Out of our desert ordeal, we become willing to have God redeem the painful expedition through the desert by applying it in another's life. Our personal Sahara becomes a gift to others. Jan Meyers's words can become our prayer:

Our daily desire can sound like this: *I hope God will tell His story through me. I hope my hard heart will soften. I hope His love shows through me in spite of myself. I hope my life will make a difference in this weary world, bringing refreshment and life to those without it. I hope to be surprised as God's glory shows up unexpectedly; I hope to have eyes to see His kindness and His humor. I hope to draw out the heart of a person with curiosity rather than alienate with my spiritual pride.*

PAIN AND PASSION

A few years into marriage, with two small children, I hit rock bottom. Everything I had ignored for years burst over me, all of my dysfunction exploded, and I had to either get out or get help. Thankfully, I ended up in a support group that turned my life around and set me on a healing path.

Thanks to the uproar and the discomfort of those years—and I do mean thanks—I began to look with deeper compassion into others' lives, listening to rather than avoiding their pain. I was surprised to learn that while I went outside the church for help for various issues, others struggled with similar problems in silence within the church. Why were we silent about the throbbing? Do we not have a God who heals, who triumphs over and in spite of our hardships and heart-slips?

TRAVELOGUE

• *Consider your past and the places Christ has led you in terms of pain and healing. How might these connect with your gifts?*

• *Consider the combination of pain and passion. Invite God into the process of identifying them and discerning how they fit together.*

There, in that incubator, God breathed life into my deadened desires, and I asked him, "What do I do with where you have taken me?" The answer I heard, over time and with growth, was "Write."

The miracle: the desert converts our pain into our passion. The problem is, we want to skirt our pain, to pretend it is not afflicting us. We don't want to look messy at church or anywhere else for that matter—isn't Christianity supposed to straighten us out and help us be nice?—so we make every effort to be "fine." It's a lie, of course; no one is "fine." But it is a lie that is reinforced in all the project-oriented work that goes on at church.

And projects are good—there is certainly work to do before Christ returns—but we lose our heart in the process of pulling together committees and filling slots on boards and rescuing programs. We say yes to vacancies because they need to be filled, not because we are called to fill them. And hopefully at some point we learn about our spiritual gifts and try to fill the slots that our gifts point to.

The only problem with "spiritual gifts" courses is that they rarely encourage us to look at our woundedness in order to find our calling. They direct us toward our passion, but we are not a passionate society, at least not with a passion that is other-directed. Our wounds, not an inventory or a chart, direct us toward our passion.

Passion is born from inevitable pain. As I recognized God's healing work in my own life, I longed to see others move in the same direction of liberty and grace. And as we allow Christ, and others, into our ache, that ache becomes a transforming process for others. God activates our gifts to align with our wounds and—as with the Israelites and with the blind man who was healed—God gains glory and others find healing. He has every intention of giving us "hope and a future" (Jeremiah 29:11), and our pain gives birth to both. What an amazing system.

OUR DEEPEST GIFT

Julian of Norwich said, "Our wounds become the womb." Those woundings become a place of formation, of new life.

This requires vulnerability: if Christ is to receive glory, then we must be willing to tell our story to others; our wounds become the place where others find companionship and freedom from their isolation. Who would think that Peter's words would find their mark when considering our pain? Yet he said, "Each one should use whatever gift he has received to serve others, faithfully administering God's grace in its various forms" (1 Peter 4:10). No doubt he was talking about our spiritual gifts, but our wounds—our deepest, most profound gifts!—show others that they are not alone, that they alone are not singled out for problems, that the camaraderie of the desert brings hope. Our pain becomes a ministering agent of God's grace and brings forth life rather than death. Nicholas Wolterstorff wrote:

> "Put your hand into my wounds," said the risen Jesus to Thomas, "and you will know who I am." The wounds of Christ are his identity. They tell us who he is. He did not lose them. . . . If sympathy for the world's wounds is not enlarged by our anguish, if love for those around us is not expanded, if gratitude for what is good does not flame up, if insight is not deepened, if commitment to what is important is not strengthened, if aching for a new day is not intensified, if hope is weakened and faith diminished, if from the experience of death comes nothing good, then death has won.

Henri Nouwen said:

> Jesus . . . [made] his own broken body the way to health, to liberation and new life. Thus like Jesus, he who proclaims liberation is called not only to care for his own wounds and the wounds of others, but also to make his wounds into a major source of his healing power.

MORE GOOD TO COME

God does not stop with magnifying wounds into healing. No, he increases his presence and love in our life through our soul Saharas. And what happens in our heart, then? Said Gary Thomas, "After God leads me through a seemingly perilous situation, I'm all His. It's the most glorious, intimate fulfillment I've ever known." What a tidy loop of love-pain-passion-calling-filling-helping-love set in motion by our desert transit, one I would never want to miss.

How perfect that we cannot traverse the desert on our own. How good that our heart must have help if we are to navigate the perils of sand-travel. How fitting that there is glory available, for God, for others, when we seek God's meaning for the sojourn.

The wilderness—meant by the enemy to hinder our heart and shift our allegiance—becomes a rich, verdant setting when we trust God and choose to find meaning in our transition and travels.

TRAVELOGUE

• *Where have you*

seen heart change in your desert?

• *In what small or large windows*

have you seen meaning for your

transition?

But what if we never understand the reason for the pain? What if we never grasp God's good purposes underlying the problems presented to us? What if we never figure out what God longed to see happen by allowing the divorce, the loss, the accident, the deteriorating health? We cannot move to bitterness in the process of seeking redemption and meaning for our desert confinement.

It is enough to know that he accompanies us on our journey. And if we are being changed, if transformation of our heart continues, if we are drawing closer to him through and as a result of our trial, then God's good purposes are finding fulfillment. Through that drawing close, God empowers us to love—and there is grace beyond our wildest imaginings.

Wilderness Response

ACCOMPANIMENT PSALM

Create in me a clean heart, O God,
And renew a steadfast spirit within me.
Do not cast me away from Your presence,
And do not take Your Holy Spirit from me.
Restore to me the joy of Your salvation,
And sustain me with a willing spirit.
Then I will teach transgressors Your ways,
And sinners will be converted to You.
PSALM 51:10-13 NASB

DESERT READING

In the time of my favor I will answer you,
   and in the day of salvation I will help you;
I will keep you and will make you
   to be a covenant for the people,
to restore the land
   and to reassign its desolate inheritances,
to say to the captives, "Come out,"
   and to those in darkness, "Be free."
ISAIAH 49:8-9

GUIDING SONG

Lord, Speak to Me

Lord, speak to me, that I may speak
In living echoes of thy tone;
As thou hast sought, so let me seek

Thine erring children lost and lone.

O strengthen me, that while I stand
Firm on the rock, and strong in thee,
I may stretch out a loving hand
To wrestlers with the troubled sea.

O teach me, Lord, that I may teach
The precious things thou dost impart;
And wing my words, that they may reach
The hidden depths of many a heart.

O fill me with thy fullness, Lord
Until my very heart o'erflow
In kindling thought and glowing word,
Thy love to tell, thy praise to show.

WORDS: FRANCES R. HAVERGAL, 1872
MUSIC: ADAPTED FROM ROBERT SCHUMANN, 1839

REMEMBER YOUR JOURNEY

- What do you want God to do in and through your heart, in and through your transition's travail?

Still Point

DEJECTION

O Father, I am in the dark,

My soul is heavy-bowed;

I send my prayer up like a lark,

Up through my vapory shroud,

To find thee,

And remind thee

I am thy child, and thou my father,

Though round me death itself should gather.

Lay thy loved hand upon my head,

Let thy heart beat in mine;

One thought from thee, when all seems dead,

Will make the darkness shine

About me

And throughout me!

And should again the dull night gather,

I'll cry again, Thou art my Father.

GEORGE MACDONALD

5

....

CHOOSING TO BE FOUND

The people who survived the sword
found grace in the wilderness.

JEREMIAH 31:2 NASB

$\mathcal{N}$ear our house was an empire, a kid's delight: acres and acres of softball diamonds, joined by chainlink fences, with a central gathering spot—the concession stand. Every night from spring's first breath through fall's final gasp, hundreds of cars pulled into parking lots, doors slammed, eager players rushed to their diamonds. Dust rose and created a filter with the bright night lights, illuminating the sky's summer haze. My son and his buddy hit Softball City as often as they could, but not to pitch and catch; their task was to find all the lost softballs and pass them to the owner. Their pay: food tokens. Cardboard pizza tastes good in only one place—Softball City—and they ate a million of 'em.

But civilization encroached on the empire, houses sprang up as farmers relinquished land for suburban sprawl. Maybe the new neighbors didn't like all those lights at night.

Softball City is now buried under another cookie-cutter housing development, one more place for people to isolate rather than congregate, to reroute their life, to shift their focus from heart to décor. Sure, the field lights are gone—replaced by hundreds of street lamps which, unlike the softball lights, never go out at night. And another collection of human beings avoids the dark, one way or another.

Much like the rest of the world. One way or another, we turn on as many lights as possible to stay out of the dark.

Spiritually speaking, we do not like darkness either. Lots of things show up in the dark, in the desert of our transition experiences. Fear, anxiety, shame, pain, longings. Most desert animals are nocturnal, avoiding daylight's triple-digit heat in favor of the nighttime's cool, brisk air. If people in the desert travel during the day, they risk dehydration, sunstroke and even death. Darkness becomes a lifesaver.

Living in the dark night of change is countercultural for us but in keeping with desert life. Even so, a tiny voice asks plaintively, What if no one finds me here, alone, in the dark? What do I do now? How do I respond to God in the dark?

WAITING IN THE DARK

Glance into any waiting room in North America, whether the airport or the doctor's office, the principal's office or the emergency room: waiting makes us edgy, tense, worried. A begging darkness descends over us as we wait. What next? Can I live through it?

We run into our own darkness while waiting, not wanting to face our ugliness or brokenness or fear, finding it hard to trust the love of a God hidden in the night times of our life.

Christians tend to believe darkness is bad, to be avoided. If we have Jesus, the Light of the World, in us, and we're supposed to be the light to others, then surely we shouldn't ever have any darkness. Shame reaches out grasping tentacles in the shadows. We shouldn't be found there, and if we are, we should just be happy, praising, rejoicing all the day. So much of our Christian culture buys into Anna's approach in *Anna and the King of Siam:* "When I feel afraid, I whistle a happy tune . . . and then I am no longer afraid."

We whistle. We pretend that the dark is really light or that it's not a big deal. The darkness isn't about sin, necessarily. It is also about broken hearts, shattered dreams, regrets, tears we haven't wept, if-only's. We say with the psalmist, "Surely the darkness will hide me and the light become night around me" (Psalm 139:11). We try to lose ourself in the dark. Or we run elsewhere to evade the gloom.

Getting lost is an age-old tactic—but God always wins our hide-and-seek games. It's a good thing, or we could grow old waiting to be found.

MOSES IN THE DARK

Moses chose to flee when faced with being found out. But perhaps he was not only running from Pharaoh, his adoptive grandfather, who intended to kill Moses for murdering an Egyptian. Perhaps Moses also ran from himself, from his failure during his first forty years to accomplish anything of meaning, for his avoidance of understanding the Hebrews' hearts. We don't know when Moses learned of his adoption and ethnicity—how long he knew that the slave nation under the cruel leadership of his adopted family was in fact kinfolk.

Somehow, he awakened one day to the injustice of it all—an Egyptian beating a Hebrew slave—and took matters into his own hands.

He connived a way out of the darkness. No time to wait for the chain of authority to act. In a moment's passion, Moses tried to outpace the darkness by killing the Egyptian. And ran for his life (Exodus 1:8—2:15).

MAKING OUR OWN LIGHT

Wrestling in my dark one morning, I queried God about the blanks on my calendar, knowing that speaking pays the mortgage but also that writing commitments and my family's heart allowed little time to speak. The marketer in me itched to jump into the dilemma wholeheartedly: spend days phoning, sending information, making new contacts, reac-

quainting myself with others. Sometimes that is precisely God's plan.
This makes the most sense for the self-employed.

Maybe *self-employed* wasn't the best term for me anymore. Maybe
God-employed would work better, though it isn't on forms I fill out. This
certainly would remind me who's in charge of my life, my home, my future. Graciously, in the midst of my panic that morning, the Lord opened
his Word and heart to me in Isaiah 50:11-12 and illuminated the dim-
ness of my faith,:

> Who among you fears the LORD
>> and obeys the word of his servant?
> Let him who walks in the dark,
>> who has no light,
> trust in the name of the LORD
>> and rely on his God.
> But now, all you who light fires
>> and provide yourselves with flaming torches,
> go, walk in the light of your fires
>> and of the torches you have set ablaze.
> This is what you shall receive from my hand:
>> You will lie down in torment.

In my nighttime shuffling, trust was an afterthought. I was lighting
my own fires, trying to provide flaming torches to throw off all the shadows, to sprint past the darkness and figure my own way out.

Who likes to face their own darkness? My darkness was fear of the future and lack of trust, wondering if God would bail us out or bail on us.
Abandonment issues cowered in the depths of my cave.

Marcie's darkness descended at the birth of her second child. This
beautiful, perfectly fashioned baby had no nerve responses from her
chin down. She lived three months.

Marcie was devastated. She was new to her church and to the women's
group when she delivered. They rallied 'round the family, bringing meals,

caring for the big sister, taking turns at the hospital, helping with bills, picking up slack. After the funeral, Marcie flung herself into the women's group, quickly accepting a leadership position. She buried her heart in volunteering. She shared bits of her pain with an older woman but largely pushed down the darkness by lighting her own torches.

Her grief finally blew out the lights totally as she approached the one-year anniversary of her daughter's birth. And all she could do was cry. But God met her in the weeping, wrapping arms around her through the warmth and presence of her new friends who had been waiting, watching for the tears.

TRAVELOGUE

• *What is the darkness for you?*

When do you "whistle"?

• *When have you made your own light in the darkness?*

• *What happens within when you try to wait out the darkness?*

My darkness seems so trivial compared to Marcie's, but I lay them side by side humbly. There are always people with more or different pain or loss. And with less. We cannot compare darkness or we end up in shame, which defeats us before we ever find the light in our cave.

This is cyclical. We run about trying to create our own light, to avoid the darkness within and without, which exacerbates the problem, furthering the darkness with fatigue, irritability, shame, guilt and typically more pain. Whatever our darkness, we have ways of piercing it with feeble attempts at light: perhaps a new friend, a new outfit, a new compensation package, a new committee, a new anything . . . We become charming, flirtatious, get prescriptions, take up a new hobby, change the pictures around on our walls, watch movies, smoke, pamper the body rather than heal the heart. We work harder, help others more. Anything, so long as we are not parked in the dark, alone, lonely, frightened. Waiting.

WAITING FOR THE LIGHT

Remember in driver's ed when they taught us not to overdrive our head-lights, not to drive so quickly that we couldn't stop to avoid something just outside the beam? The principle is the same in transition: moving too fast, we overdrive our headlights and end up in the dark, at best, or in a disaster, at worst. Rather than make our own light, our only real op-tion is to wait for the Light. To sit on the ash heap with Job, bewildered by the dark but willing to stay there until God comes.

Darkness is not about self-help but about needing a match that we cannot strike on our own. God must flip the switch for us and illuminate our cave. He calls us to wait there for him. To sit in the darkness, to open our heart to our longings; our brokenness; our disappointments with God, self, others; our hopes, unfulfilled by definition.

The wilderness of transition is a spiritually and emotionally evocative environment—it calls out our heart, inviting us to be found. This means residing in a very uncomfortable place. Typically we skirt our pain, our brokenness. We don't want to be untidy! We want to be fine. And that's legitimate and human.

It just doesn't work.

HIDING

While on staff in a church, Lynn talked with a woman who served on a prominent committee. The woman lamented her inability to fulfill some of the tasks. Lynn, knowing of the land mines the woman had jumped recently, said compassionately, "The bottom fell out of your life this year; don't worry about the committee now."

The woman stiffened into a "how dare you" posture, refusing to speak to Lynn for the rest of Lynn's tenure. She couldn't stand to be considered incompetent, messy, broken.

It's so frightening to think of being discovered, by others, by God, by ourself! Our defenses go up, and we hide our heart and our needs. But somehow we have to learn to let God find us in our messiness. The wilderness is good about that.

God sees us when we try to disappear. He has always been a seeking God, coming to find us: "Adam, where are you?" he asked, when Adam cowered behind some fig leaves in hopes of going unnoticed by the lover of his soul (Genesis 3:1-9). Fat chance. And Elijah, full of dark discouragement, hid in a cave until God found him and asked, "Elijah, buddy, whatchadoin' in a cave?" (1 Kings 19:9, my rendering). Elijah answered, "I have been very zealous for the LORD God Almighty. The Israelites have . . . put your prophets to death with the sword. I am the only one left, and now they are trying to kill me too." Caught in his fear, caught in the cave, Elijah could only moan. And God responded, "Go out and stand on the mountain in the presence of the LORD, for the LORD is about to pass by" (1 Kings 19:10-11). God came for Elijah.

Psalm 139 is a song of great comfort, while uncomfortable in all of God's knowing. We cannot disappear into the darkness; we cannot outdistance God. Verses 7-10 say:

Where can I go from your Spirit?
>Where can I flee from your presence?
If I go up to the heavens, you are there;
>if I make my bed in the depths, you are there.
If I rise on the wings of the dawn,
>if I settle on the far side of the sea,
even there your hand will guide me,
>your right hand will hold me fast.

God is not confined by darkness, nor repelled by ours. The good news is, in verse 12, that "even the darkness will not be dark to you; the night will shine like the day, for darkness is as light to you." He will find us. Our best—our only—response is not hiding, but leaning.

LEANING

Rather than running or disappearing, leaning is our saving grace in the dark caves of change. Transitions, meant to move us away from stubborn independence, become perfect opportunities to learn to lean. The Jerusalem Bible translates Isaiah 50:10 in this way:

> Let anyone who fears Yahweh among you
> listen to the voice of his servant!
> Whoever walks in darkness,
> and has no light shining for him,
> let him trust in the name of Yahweh,
> let him lean on his God.

Leaning. What a concept in our autonomous worlds. Leaning goes against our grain. After all, we're expected to do all things well, alone. Group projects are great in school, but in the real world, the market place, it's every woman for herself. Competition is fierce, and we'd better edge everyone else out. Leaning is not politically correct, whether at work or home.

My husband came into my office one morning, knowing I was desperately fighting deadlines. "How can I help?" I drew a blank. "Anywhere?" Nothing. The house was trashed, laundry piled high, the cupboard bare and not a whiff of dinner in the air. But there was nothing he could do to help. A sad look washed over him. "You've worked me out of being needed, Jane," he said.

We've been weaned on slogans like "I am woman—hear me roar!" and "Never underestimate the power of a woman." And in many arenas we need to be strong, self-sufficient. Still, I've done about enough roaring.

Is it not the same with the church? We are not encouraged to be needy, to lean. Which fits perfectly, since we are wired for running, whether churches, businesses or houses, committees, agendas or programs. Part of the fallout from the Fall was control: we want to drive (Genesis 3:6, 16). We do not want to sit around and wait for God to show up. We do not want anyone else to lead; we want the steering wheel.

How do we wait in the darkness and learn to "lean on our God"? My friend says, "Jane, lean into your anger." I don't get it. She tries again, "Let yourself be angry—give yourself permission. Stay in that feeling. Let it bring you to God, to your deepest longings."

Part of the problem is misunderstanding the darkness: it is inefficient unless embraced as a place to rest. Leaning means rest, repose, to let another support you, bear your weight, carry you, receive your anxiety, hold your pain. But what if the other person shifts and we lose our balance? How horrible if someone had to literally catch us. Or what if that person drops us, or turns on us, or moves entirely and we fall over? We don't want to be disappointed or hurt in our leaning.

Once I traveled ninety minutes for a meeting. A group member, a dear friend, called us there. "The

TRAVELOGUE

• *Describe your times of waiting in the dark. What happened?*

• *Where does your heart go when you think about leaning on another—not carrying your own weight anymore?*

• *When have you tried leaning and been wounded? What would it look like to lean now?*

ambulance is coming for my husband, I found him lying on the floor, I won't be coming to the meeting." And she hung up. When the rest of our group gathered, we phoned around for the correct hospital, then carpooled over, surrounding her in the ER with prayers and love and a snack. At another crisis, she didn't call. When we asked why she'd gone through the pain alone, she said, "I was afraid you'd get in your car and drive over."

Of course. Or at least prayed her through the darkness. But she speaks for us all: who wants to ooze raw pain around others, or be needy? And we certainly don't want to inconvenience anyone, even people we dearly love.

But leaning—on God, on the primary supports God places around us—becomes our candle in the cave. Our choice to be found means learning to lean on the invisible God. Even so, at the bottom of our darkness-avoiding techniques is once again a lack of trust.

MERCY IN THE DARK

The bottom line: we don't always believe that God will find us in the dark, that he will choose to rescue us. But waiting out our transitions in the night is a gift.

> God's name is Mercy. We see our darkness as a prized possession because it drives us into the heart of God. Without mercy our darkness would plunge us into despair—and for some, self-destruction. Time alone with God reveals the unfathomable depths of the poverty of our spirit. . . . In a sudden and luminous moment we realize that we are being accosted by Mercy and embraced even before we lay hold of ourselves.

Last night, pain and anger filled me over a parent-child issue. Finally I whispered, "Find me, God. Find me." The tears pressed close, but so did God. I could sense him nearby, within. Mercy found and held me. The problem didn't disappear, but the intense anger and hurt and despair lessened.

Being found isn't an elaborate process. We don't have to memorize anything or learn a new behavior-language or stick stars on a chart. We need only cry out, in our helplessness, our lostness, "Find me." Choosing to be found brings the light of God into the darkness of our desert. It's as easy as leaning on our Daddy's chest.

Because of the tender mercy of our God,

With which the Sunrise from on high will visit us,

To shine upon those who sit in darkness and the shadow of death,

To guide our feet into the way of peace.

(Luke 1:78-79 NASB)

He waits for us to call.

JESUS AND THE SHADOW OF DEATH

On the night betrayal's breath drew near, Jesus took the bread and blessed it, giving thanks—knowing the coming darkness, the treachery, the approaching agony. He knew that his body would soon be broken, symbolized in the tearing apart of the bread. He knew his blood would soon spill out. And still he gave thanks.

This is not Jesus putting on a happy face. This is Jesus, seeing the people he loved dearly sitting at the table with him—seeing them, he looked past his brokenness to the coming joy. He knew that out of his brokenness would be life, our life, our salvation.

He let God find him in the darkness. And God brought life out of death.

And so the Lord invites us to choose to be found. To wait out the darkness. To wait with the pain of betrayal, the brokenness, the despair, the fear, and to let God find us.

> TRAVELOGUE
>
> • *Listen, in the*
>
> *darkness, until you hear God*
>
> *calling your name.*
>
> *Invite him to find you.*

Just as God called Adam, so he calls us. Do you hear his longing voice, "Daughter, where are you?" Just whisper, "Find me, Lord. Find me." And being found, you will find grace in the wilderness.

Wilderness Response

ACCOMPANIMENT PSALM

How long, O LORD? Will you forget me forever?
How long will you hide your face from me?
How long must I wrestle with my thoughts
and every day have sorrow in my heart?
How long will my enemy triumph over me?

Look on me and answer, O LORD my God.
Give light to my eyes, or I will sleep in death;
my enemy will say, "I have overcome him,"
and my foes will rejoice when I fall.

But I trust in your unfailing love;
my heart rejoices in your salvation.
I will sing to the LORD,
for he has been good to me.

PSALM 13

DESERT READING

"For I know the plans I have for you," declares the LORD, "plans
to prosper you and not to harm you, plans to give you hope and a
future. Then you will call upon me and come and pray to me, and
I will listen to you. You will seek me and find me when you seek
me with all your heart. I will be found by you," declares the LORD,
"and will bring you back from captivity."

JEREMIAH 29:11-14

GUIDING SONG

Near to the Heart of God

There is a place of quiet rest,
Near to the heart of God,
A place where sin cannot molest
Near to the heart of God.

Chorus:
O Jesus, blest Redeemer
Sent from the heart of God,
Hold us who wait before Thee
Near to the heart of God.

There is a place of comfort sweet,
Near to the heart of God,
A place where we our Savior meet,
Near to the heart of God.

There is a place of full release,
Near to the heart of God,
A place where all is joy and peace,
Near to the heart of God.

WORDS AND MUSIC: CLELAND B. MCAFEE, 1903

REMEMBER YOUR JOURNEY

- In the wilderness we can light our own torches or learn to lean. Journal about your heart choice for the darkness.

Still Point

Solitude is thus the place of purification and transformation,

the place of the great struggle and the great encounter.

Solitude is not simply a means to an end.

Solitude is its own end.

It is the place where Christ remodels us in his own image

and frees us from the victimizing compulsions of the world.

Solitude is the place of our salvation.

HENRI NOUWEN, *THE WAY OF THE HEART*

6

········

CHOOSING TO FLOURISH

Be strong in the grace that is in Christ Jesus.

2 TIMOTHY 2:1

$\mathcal{B}$ig malls, heavily populated areas and huge frigid stores lure some people. I absolutely dread shopping there. We have a glitzy supermarket near us which I frequent only when out of vitals like coffee, milk and fruit. After parking and hiking across a large parking lot, I wrestle a cart away from a thousand others. Inside, the empire totally overwhelms my senses and instantly exhausts me. Colors, brilliant, polished, accost my eyes; the scents of fried chicken and fresh-baked bread compete with the aroma of the designer coffee. Fortunately I don't smell the sushi bar.

A bank and teller machine offer quick fixes to pocketbook problems, and there's a change counter for the distressed—the machine sucks up all the coins found in the sofa and the washing machine, counts them for a fee and spits out a receipt for the money to apply toward groceries. For those feeling the need of medication, there's the pharmacy. Did I mention the seasonal aisles and the floral department?

When possible, I shop the little store with its wares still in boxes. With four aisles, my choices are simplified. I can think. It's much better for my soul and my attitude.

It is hard to think, hard to feel our heart and sustain honest growth in a world where there is such a visual, visceral display set before us regularly. The simplicity of the desert, its sparse surroundings, allows us to move away from the sensory onslaught of a consumers' paradise to the place where flourishing must begin if we are to endure and thrive: the internal recesses of our soul.

As Moses found when fleeing the angry pharaoh, as the Israelites found in their exodus, the paucity of the desert gives pause to our soul. Without the wilderness of change, we might never have to look at the direction of our heart and life. So God lets us encounter the hot, dry desert, lets us move into a place where we are not distracted by all the hustle and bustle about us. He lets us go to the wilderness. Karen Mains writes:

> The amazing thing about wilderness wanderings is that our souls often flourish in parched and arid terrain; whereas when we are comfortable, protected by familiarity and surrounded by the pleasures and treasures of home, our souls tend to languish. . . . Moses flees to the wilderness of Midian to preserve his life, but in God's amazing provision, the wilderness preserves Moses' soul. It is in the desert that Moses begins to comprehend the national identity of the Hebrews. More importantly, he comes to know the One who is the God of the Hebrew people. In the wilderness there is time enough for transformation.

Through transitions, God disrupts the "earn money . . . gain favor . . . buy a house . . . settle down . . . live content as creators of our own good fortune" cycle.

We don't have to be a cactus to grow in the desert, but failure to thrive ultimately means death. Flourishing in the desert is a distinct possibility—if we are willing to reconsider what it means to be fruitful.

THE DIVIDING LINE

"What lies behind us and what lies before us are tiny matters compared to what lies within us," penned Ralph Waldo Emerson, and what lies within us may remain entirely hidden without the dividing line of transition, without the identity crisis so frequent in times of change.

A transition becomes a type of equator, separating the hemispheres in our life: before the accident, after the divorce, we say. There is the way life was (or at least the way we prefer to remember it, though we may alter our memories, like retouching old photos, adding color, taking away glare) and the way life will be. The temptation is to either look back, holding onto the past, or to keep looking ahead.

TRAVELOGUE

• *In what ways have*

you bided your time, living on

the equator, waiting for the end of

the wilderness, rather than living

fully in the now?

"When this is over." "When I am well." "When my child returns." "When my husband quits drinking." "When I get a new job." "When I finally conceive."

And for a time, all we can do is get through, with life on hold. The grief and shock of change mandate marking time for a period. But the temptation is to not really live for the duration of the desert. Writes Manette Ansay, a pianist with a brilliant future who began experiencing paralyzing pain, ultimately abandoning her career:

> I was biding my time, waiting for the day when I'd see the right doctor, find the right medication, make a full recovery. As a result, I experienced my day-to-day life with a curious sense of distance. It was as if I was watching myself, or a person like myself, someone who was holding my place in the world, keeping up appearances until my real self could return.

At a commercial foods convention, an industry player hired one of our friends to perform a robot routine. Having perfected robotic move-

ment and vacant eyes, he applied pancake makeup, polished his shoes
and attached a cord to himself to look like he was plugged into a power
outlet in the booth. He spent hours gliding about the display, showing
no reaction to visitors who speculated, "Do you think he's real?" "He acts
real." "He can't be real—look at his eyes."

I think about his robot when considering life in the desert of transitions. It's so easy to go through the motions, pretending life doesn't
hurt, continuing to serve and give and move about our individual
booths. But within, our heart is dying, and our vacant eyes acknowledge the truth: that somehow we have failed, or life or God has failed
us. The desert is not about failure, unless it's heart failure. To live—to
blossom—in the sands of change, we have to understand the cycling
of the seasons.

RECOGNIZING THE SEASON

I don't pretend to know much about agriculture, though my grandparents owned a farm in Tennessee and my father-in-law does some farming
now. But I do understand the possibility of overfarming the soil, deplet-
ing the earth of essential nutrients and destroying the chemical balance
necessary to good plant growth. One remedy for soil depletion is dormancy, letting the fields lie, inactive, unplanted and seemingly unpro-
ductive for a season.

Dormancy. It looks a lot like rest, doesn't it? Resting from seasons of
heavy tilling, fertilizing and high productivity. The original word actually means to sleep. But I think even *dormancy* is a misnomer, because
dormancy feels like nothing is happening. Perhaps not, at least not vis-
ibly; after all, nothing blooms, no ripe heads of grain sway on golden
stems, no corn glows on vivid green stalks, no soybeans cling to the
ground, no cotton cloaks the earth in white. This is the problem with
the value we place on high-visibility productivity versus the underground nature of replenishment. Though fruit is not apparent, life continues and deepens invisibly.

Maybe there is truly no such season as dormancy, in the soil or in our soul. The earth's life cycle includes four seasons. Spring is a reaching, blooming season, running into summer's heat and sun and fruit. Fall is a shedding, decomposing time that actually prepares a nutritious compost for the soil. And winter. Ah, the equivalent of desert barrenness. The place where all that is perceptible is the starkness of death: the bare trees, the brown grass (if the stubble is not covered by snow), the gaunt, crisp stems of perennials whose beauty has gone beneath to preserve their future. Below the surface, life is being restored: roots stretch, bulbs are nurtured, plants and soil find rest.

Perhaps transition's desert is just that for us: a season of repletion, of rest, of burrowing underground to preserve and strengthen our life for the future. Change is a season of the soul. Surely the desert is the ideal place for us to consider what growth and good might possibly be happening for us right now. But we must first reconsider how we define fruit.

REDEFINING FRUIT

How does fruit look in the wilderness? Not like apples and rhododendrons, for sure. In "former days," days when we were able to keep the pace of the rest of the world, able to run the race (albeit often robotically), we believed fruit to be about our involvements, our extracurriculars, the people helped, the hospitality offered, the classes taught, even the prayers prayed. It isn't fair to expect this of ourself or even of God while in the midst of a season of change. The desert is still a place of fruitfulness—it is simply a different fruit, a different purpose.

One of the ways we *live,* rather than just hold our place in line, is by asking the question, what fruit will I expect? In what will I be involved? Can we take ourself off the productivity hook, the external involvement spoke, and let God have his way in our heart for the season?

The desert asks who we are becoming. The fruit of the wilderness, rather than coming from external showy flowers, may be found in Galatians 5:22-23. Interestingly, none of the Spirit-fruit involves serving

TRAVELOGUE

• *What feeling does*
"dormancy" have for you?
When was the last time someone
gave you permission to rest and
not produce? What happens
within when you consider
that possibility?

• *What fruit have you—or*
others—expected of yourself in
the past?

• *What does trust look like for you*
in the wilderness?

on committees or running soup kitchens. Instead, these fruits are character qualities growing from a heart made fertile by God's loving presence, not activities or involvements: "But the fruit of the Spirit is love, joy, peace, patience, kindness, goodness, faithfulness, gentleness and self-control. Against such things there is no law."

This is not to say that we relinquish all involvements that do not focus on ourself and our soul-preservation, becoming narcissistic and narrow. But rather, we carefully examine our conceptions of "success" concerning the wilderness. There are seasons when we are less available for others because God has work to do in our heart and circumstances keep us pressed against the wall of reality and our human limitations.

During Jesus' forty days in the wilderness (Luke 4:1-12), he wasn't winning disciples and stocking the food pantry or even healing people. The wilderness was a battle for his soul, and flourishing meant trust. Trusting God's calling, God's plan, God's power to protect. Relying on God's Word to do battle with the enemy, who would rather destroy us, leaving our bones to bleach out in the hot sun.

Flourishing in the wilderness looks like an ever-deepening cycle of dependency and trust.

Respecting the Life Process of the Desert: Adaptation

Recognizing where we are—whoa, I think this is a desert!—means we eventually must cry out to God, "I can't make it! I know nothing about living in all this hot sand. I am afraid I will die here." We must learn the way of the desert and how life endures such severity.

To the practiced eye, deserts are far from barren or lifeless. Plant life, though it may be few and far between, continues because it knows how to seek water, whether spreading broad roots or sinking twenty- to thirty-foot taproots to access underground water.

So must we, if we are to benefit from, rather than just tolerate, our transitions. We must put ourself in places where we are nurtured, our parched soul watered, our life tended by others who love us and care for us.

If reaching water means solitude, we must find space. If silence nurtures, allowing us to hear God's voice again, we wait for God to still our anxious heart. God's Word rejuvenates, so we gulp. But we do more than gulp, we savor that living water, letting it seep into our mind and heart like a long, gentle spring rain on the desert floor. We cannot expect to intersect with the God of the wilderness, to experience transformation, without seeking water.

For Bernard of Clairvaux, a monk and reformer who lived from 1090 to 1153, "The secret of . . . spiritual vision was the practice of *contemplation*—by which he trained his soul to stay focused on the overwhelming goodness and the eternal purposes of God above all else." This spiritual practice kept his heart by looking at God and at eternal good. This is another way to redefine fruit: Even though we cannot see what good is going on at present—we cannot see souls being saved or political rulers and regimes changed by Christ's presence—we trust God for fruit in the future.

These desert disciplines will not only get us through the long valley, they will help us flourish in the wilderness.

RELEASING OURSELVES

At thirty, Celia really thought she'd be married. All her life she'd looked forward to having a husband, being a joyful wife, sharing hospitality, raising children. And though her longings are strong, her faith is deep. During this season of singleness, she gives herself over to God.

"This is a time when I can help others," she says. "I wouldn't be able to spend a week at someone's hospital bedside if I were married and raising children. I wouldn't be able to travel with my work or invest so much time in the church. I would still have an impact, but it would be different. So I am giving my life to the kingdom. When God brings a husband, it will be wonderful. But here's where God has me. So God can use me here, now, even in the midst of my unmet longings."

This is no glib pronouncement; Celia has wept internally through friends' weddings, wrangled with God in the wilderness about his plans for her. She has worked too hard at times, at the cost of her health and her relationship with God.

But she has released herself to God, to whatever his plans may be, to his goodness, for now and for the future—knowing that somehow brokenness today turns into tomorrow's wholeness and that God's good purposes for us will not be thwarted but rather enhanced by our wilderness sojourn. Submitting to that goodness is a fast track to thriving in the wilderness. Nancy Guthrie writes:

> Because I believe God's plans for me are better than I can plan for myself, rather than run away from the path he has set before me, I want to run toward it. I don't want to try to change God's mind— his thoughts are perfect. I want to think his thoughts. I don't want to change God's timing—his timing is perfect. I want the grace to accept his timing. I don't want to change God's plan—his plan is perfect. I want to embrace his plan and see how he is glorified through it.
>
> Even when life's imperfections seem so far out of line with God's best,

desert flourishing is an option when we embrace God there. Look at El Niño. In 1998, because of unusual weather patterns, the rainfall in desert regions created lush, vibrant flowers. So much so that, in the Mojave Desert, rarely seen plants became the basis for coffee table books and their fragrances formed new perfume lines.

Can our life flourish regardless of the harsh terrain, blowing sand, heat and seemingly relentless nothingness? Our choices remain: to let the soil of our life become bitter and barren or to open ourself to God's goodness in the midst of things we do not understand, receiving all that he longs to plant within us.

> God does not care . . . whether I am happy or not. What God cares about, with all the power of God's holy being, is . . . not just the continuation of my breath and the health of my cells—

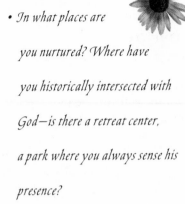

TRAVELOGUE

- *In what places are you nurtured? Where have you historically intersected with God—is there a retreat center, a park where you always sense his presence?*

- *How have you accessed water in the past? What adaptations do you need to make for desert blossoming?*

- *Where is God inviting you to relinquish yourself to his goodness? How do you resist? Now where do you go with the process?*

but the quality of my life, the scope of my life, the heft and zest of my life. . . . [The] fear of death always turns into fear of life, into a stingy, cautious way of living that is not really living at all. . . . [T]o follow Jesus means going beyond the limits of our own comfort and safety. It means receiving our lives as gifts instead of guarding them as . . . possessions.

ONE DAY

One day, the desert will turn into a flourishing land. Awaiting certain calamity for his people, Habakkuk beautifully depicts the essence of living on the equator, the dividing line of before and after. He is a picture of choosing to flourish in the midst of transitions. Habakkuk 3:17-18 reads:

> Though the fig tree does not bud
>> and there are no grapes on the vines,
> though the olive crop fails
>> and the fields produce no food,
> though there are no sheep in the pen
>> and no cattle in the stalls,
> yet I will rejoice in the LORD,
>> I will be joyful in God my Savior.

Until the day when the desert blooms, we will let God define our fruitfulness and trust him for our heart, living fully in this land of in-between. Choosing to flourish in the desert becomes a junction with God's divine, unmerited favor. A grace point.

Wilderness Response

ACCOMPANIMENT PSALM

Blessed is the man
who does not walk in the counsel of the wicked
or stand in the way of sinners
or sit in the seat of mockers.
But his delight is in the law of the LORD,
and on his law he meditates day and night.
He is like a tree planted by streams of water,
which yields its fruit in season
and whose leaf does not wither.
Whatever he does prospers.

PSALM 1:1-2

DESERT READING

Remember how the LORD your God led you all the way in the desert these forty years, to humble you and to test you in order to know what was in your heart, whether or not you would keep his commands. He humbled you, causing you to hunger and then feeding you with manna, which neither you nor your fathers had known, to teach you that man does not live on bread alone but on every word that comes from the mouth of the LORD. Your clothes did not wear out and your feet did not swell during these forty years. Know then in your heart that as a man disciplines his son, so the LORD your God disciplines you.

Observe the commands of the LORD your God, walking in his ways and revering him. For the LORD your God is bringing you into a good land—a land with streams and pools of water, with

springs flowing in the valleys and hills; a land with wheat and bar-
ley, vines and fig trees, pomegranates, olive oil and honey; a land
where bread will not be scarce and you will lack nothing. . . .

When you have eaten and are satisfied, praise the LORD your
God for the good land he has given you.

DEUTERONOMY 8:2-10

GUIDING SONG

Grace Greater Than Our Sins

Marvelous grace of our loving Lord,
Grace that exceeds our sin and our guilt!
Yonder on Calvary's mount outpoured,
There where the blood of the Lamb was spilt.

Refrain:
Grace, grace, God's grace,
Grace that will pardon and cleanse within;
Grace, grace, God's grace,
Grace that is greater than all our sin!

Sin and despair, like the seawaves cold,
Threaten the soul with infinite loss;
Grace that is greater, yes, grace untold,
Points to the refuge, the mighty cross.

Dark is the stain that we cannot hide,
What can avail to wash it away?
Look! There is flowing a crimson tide,
Brighter than snow you may be today.

Marvelous, infinite, matchless grace,

Freely bestowed on all who believe!
You that are longing to see his face,
Will you this moment his grace receive?
WORDS: JULIA H. JOHNSTON, 1911
MUSIC: DANIEL B. TOWNER, 1910

REMEMBER YOUR JOURNEY

- Invite God to define flourishing for you in this season. Journal about your hesitations and doubts as well as your hopes.

Still Point

Turn your eyes [from the allure of this world and its pride],

and be caught up instead in the Glorious One

who draws us to himself on high.

Let us follow after the desire that is already kindled in our hearts. . . .

It is the fire of holiness that is aroused in us

by the Spirit of him who whispers,

"I will kiss you with the kisses of my mouth!"

BERNARD OF CLAIRVAUX

7

....

CHOOSING TO FOCUS

And the God of all grace, who called you to his eternal glory in Christ,

after you have suffered a little while, will himself restore you and make you strong,

firm and steadfast. To him be the power for ever and ever. Amen.

1 PETER 5:10-11

A gray day. Gray water, gray skies, gray heart. Glancing out the window, a flash of red in a gray, bare-boned tree caught my eye, dazzling against the somber background. For a long time, I watched the cardinal perched on the finger-slim branch, my hands stilled over the keyboard, my heart quieted. Something shifted inside me then: a blind cranked open over the eye of my soul, and light streamed in between the slats.

Much of life is about choice: about choosing to live while we're alive, not being half present and just trudging through. Choosing our focal point becomes a discipline of the desert. I could wallow in the worries surrounding me, letting them seep inside, lodge, expand and solidify like a gray cement block, absorbing all the room in my lungs and heart and mind. I could focus on the problems, the doubts, the what-ifs. I could easily focus on the past, the pain, the people who hurt or troubled me.

• When have you had

to "make nice," avoid talking

about problems, chosen to

lip-sync? What messages did

you receive in the past that

created this tendency?

If I wanted to live gray. This is my natural bent; this is where my mind goes without effort. But in a world where the brilliant robe of a cardinal flashes through naked trees, where sunshine shoots like a flare off the rippling water, where even now baby green leaves dot the tips of branches—in a world shot through with glory, I will not live gray. I will miss God if I live gray.

Even in the bleak wilderness of change, we can learn to tether our thoughts, hook them up, as Paul admonishes, to "whatever is true . . . noble . . . right . . . pure . . . lovely . . . admirable—if anything is excellent or praiseworthy" (Philippians 4:8).

But choosing to focus does not mean lip-syncing, "It is well, it is well with my soul." We do not pretend that bad things never happen, that every moment is jam-packed with joy and beauty; there is no choice about focusing if there is no darkness. Choosing to focus honestly is impossible if we have not grappled with our pain, faced our darkness, ventured into the yawning void of the wilderness.

MOSES' FOCUS

Forty years after Moses killed the Egyptian and fled, God met him on the mountain, in the blazing bush encounter. Even with such an amazing display of God's glory, Moses could not take his eyes off his own doubts and insecurities. Perhaps his past haunted him in the immediacy of God's calling; perhaps he feared failure in light of his previous performance. His queries flew at the Lord, his what-ifs cluttering the air.

"Who am I, that I should go to Pharaoh and bring the Israelites out of Egypt?" God's answer had nothing to do with Moses; the Lord redirected

Moses' attention to himself: "I will be with you" (Exodus 3:11-12).

"Yeah, but who are you?" Moses' actual words were, "Suppose I go to the Israelites and say to them, 'The God of your fathers has sent me to you,' and they ask me, 'What is his name?' Then what shall I tell them?" (Exodus 3:13).

God reminded him, "I AM WHO I AM," the ancient name for God, the God of Abraham, Isaac and Jacob (Exodus 3:14). This is the God who has been and will be forever. Again, the focus shifts from Moses' insecurity to God's sufficiency (Exodus 3:13-15).

The Lord's further reassurances left Moses unconvinced. After God divulged all the wonders and rescuing he would perform, Moses said, "What if they do not believe me or listen to me and say, 'The LORD did not appear to you'?" (Exodus 4:1). God answered with live action footage—Moses' rod turned into a snake, the snake turned back into a staff, his hand turned leprous, his hand was healed. It's all about what God would do. And if that wasn't enough, if the people didn't believe those signs, the One God would turn the Nile into blood.

But Moses still thought about himself. "What if I screw it up? Get all tongue-tied?" (my paraphrase). "O Lord, I have never been eloquent, neither in the past nor since you have spoken to your servant. I am slow of speech and tongue" (Exodus 4:10).

God tempered his response with compassion but left no doubt about his sovereignty. He is in charge of people's mouths, their words and their hearing. "Now go; I will help you speak and will teach you what to say" (Exodus 4:11-12).

This should have been enough. But Moses hadn't truly looked up at God yet, hadn't grasped the power of his relationship with the Lord of lords, of being called and commissioned and given a task to do and everything required to complete that task. This calling wasn't about Moses at all. It was about God.

The goodness of all this poor focusing—all the what-ifs, the what-about-me questions—is that when God delivers there is no doubt in our mind that it was God. There is no possibility we can claim credit for the wonders, because God's glory and power eradicate our inadequacy. We rub our worry stones for a while, stew in our juices. Then our focus is all the clearer when the veil lifts and we see his heart, breaking for his people in bondage, determined to deliver.

Our vision is dim, this side of heaven, our eyes blinded by the day-to-day existence and the safety curtain obscuring God's face from us. One day we will see clearly, face to face. In the meantime, our focus must be God's heart for us, God's future for us, God's keeping of us.

BENEFITS OF FOCUS

Knowing God's heart and longings helps immensely when we consider transferring our focus from ourself to God, reaping the benefits of re-training our eyes.

God-centered. I loved the order of a hymnal I scanned: hymn selections were clustered under categories, moving from "The Upward Look" to "The Inward Look" to "The Outward Look." It's a good pattern for our life. In the midst of the desert, looking at ourself only, we become truncated by quicksand. If we only look outward, at activities and involvements and other people's lives, like the tumbleweed we will never have roots or depth. But if we look first at God, at his character, person and attributes, then our desert becomes a God-centered place, and he is able to inform our "inward looking" (which is essential) and keep us from self-centeredness by moving us to "outward looking."

Self-pity flees. Facing monetary devastation in their business, Phil and Carol refinanced their house, trimmed every possible expenditure, stopped receiving a salary and grimly set about settling their debts. The slow, grueling process wore them down.

Carol said, "My thoughts ran in a circle, like, 'How can this be? We have worked hard all our lives, never owed anyone an overdue dime, and now in our sixties we face financial ruin.'" Finally, deep in prayer, she sensed God at her side, beckoning her past her self-pity into deep intercession for others in financial straits. Bowed in humility, the Lord began to heal her wounds as she focused not just on her needs and desperation but also on the pain of others. The black despair departed and joy crept in slowly, like the dawn.

Provides perspective. One couple spent the last year battling for the wife's very life with the discovery of aggressive breast cancer. Her cancer markers were down, the treatment appeared successful, and they began to breathe deeply again. He gripped his wife's hand tightly and held it up. "This is what's important. We have each other. We have God."

The wilderness has a clarifying quality: distilling out the nonessentials and, if we are listening carefully, showing us what is worth battling over.

Avoids obsessing. Focusing keeps us from obsessing about the worry or anguish in front of or behind us. This does not mean invoking a mindless, worthless chant like, "I will not think about this, I will not think about this." Changing our focus in midstream means deliberately choosing something to replace it.

Again this fall, when I looked ahead at my calendar, I catered to panic for too many hours. Fear of the future again swallowed my soul. Finally, I opened the Scriptures and let God access my mind and heart. Finally. Choosing to focus not on the wilderness but on the Lord of the wilderness, I fell asleep with the final phrases to Psalm 28 enveloping me. "Be their shepherd also, and carry them forever" (Psalm 28:9 NASB). When I awakened in the arms of the Shepherd, my heart sang a different tune, and my thinking moved along the lines of "holy, holy, holy."

> Since, then, you have been raised with Christ, set your hearts on things above, where Christ is seated at the right hand of God. Set your minds on things above, not on earthly things. For you died, and your life is now hidden with Christ in God. When Christ, who is your life, appears, then you also will appear with him in glory. (Colossians 3:1-4)

If I have died in Christ, then the One who raises the dead can take

care of my earthly worries. And I will try to remember to set my eyes and
my heart on him.

DISTRACTING OUR FOCUS

Knowing the One who created us, who lived and died and rose again for
us, knowing that this God is capable of handling our daily pain and
chaos helps. But it's easy to shift our focus away from God's care and
goodness and into unhealthy places.

Others as irritants. In transition, irritability rises and our proclivity
is to blame. The smallest annoyance about another may make us crazy,
as though all our nerve endings sit exposed on the outside of our skin
and the slightest brush against us makes us jumpy.

Ourselves. When Cherie's husband left her for another woman, he
left a mountain of bills and three children. In detached moments she is
surprised by his continued cruelty, but mostly she is furious. Genuine
anguish makes it hard to invite others to share our life, joy and sorrow.

Preoccupation is normal in places of deep aching. However, the enemy wants to keep us there, to rob us not only of our present but of our
future, our joy and the healing waiting in the wings—not to mention
life-giving friends.

The past. Our mind capably re-creates a panoramic view of our past,
where we endlessly replay the pain, the mistakes, another's treatment of
us. How tempting to stay focused on the past and its valid pain. But
chronic anger and unforgiveness debilitate us; receiving forgiveness and
in turn offering it, letting the past create new life instead of death within,
frees us from the slavery of the past.

Regret in retrospect. Reading back through some journals, shame en-
gulfs me over words spoken hastily, irretrievably, over actions quick and
damaging, without thought. If only I'd moved more slowly there, more
deliberately here, then the damage would have been controlled or min-
imized, rather than seeming like a spreading wildfire.

Shame is one of the most debilitating weapons in Satan's arsenal; it steals up from behind, waiting to halt us like a stun gun. When I run into past incidents where the flood of shame rises in me, I have to stop, remember the cross—where Christ hung without shame for my sake—and push shame back (Hebrews 12:1-2). When God forgives, he drops our sin into the bottom of the sea (Micah 7:18-19). Retrospect is helpful when it

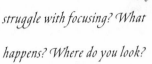

TRAVELOGUE

• *When do you most struggle with focusing? What happens? Where do you look?*

• *Where have you been most tempted to lose your focus?*

leads us to mercy and maturity—rather than immobilizing us with shame.

Comparisons. The same way people compare cars, houses and salaries, it is tempting to compare God's blessings and presence in our life with his work in others' lives. Occasionally one of our children says, "You didn't do that with [a sibling]!" But children are different, needing different approaches based on temperament, age, situation and self-esteem level.

God must take this into account with us, as well, when he acts differently in our life. How natural to compare, whining like covetous kids, "Why is God doing this for you and not me?" Desert comparisons poison our soul. Since we know that God shows no partiality (James 2:1-12), it helps to see this tendency as a longing, perhaps, for perfection, for heaven, moving back to God's presence with our heart.

The visible. Not only do we live in a world of comparison, that world tempts us to believe that what we see is all there is. The media reinforces this every time we open our eyes. We focus on the externals and ignore what God longs to do within and through us. This desert voyage is about the eternal, not the external. The psalmist asks, "I look up to the mountains; does my strength come from mountains? No, my strength comes from GOD, who made heaven, and earth, and mountains" (Psalm 121:1-2 The Message). We don't look around us for answers and hope, we look to the One who made our surroundings.

FOCUS ON WHAT?

When Rich and I were in seminary, working two jobs, living with a woman who had Alzheimer's disease in exchange for room and board, and raising a newborn, we began to memorize hymns. Not because we needed something else to do but because we wanted to focus on God's goodness in our life, especially in a time when we were stretched to the limit. Our first (and possibly only) selection was "Great Is Thy Faithfulness." How humbling to focus on fact: he has stayed faithful to us, in spite of our wandering ways and inattention and doubt.

Sometimes, though, I cannot sing that hymn without anger—at a current situation or someone who troubles me or a seeming nonanswer from God. Then I have to focus on God's presence in the midst of my problems and pain, his provisions in the past. No, it doesn't take away the pain—but it takes away pain's debilitating power.

In the midst of the barrens, we remember that God's "compassions never fail" (Lamentations 3:22-24) but are renewed daily as we focus on him. We look at the life around us, at the brilliance of children, the miracle of love or the astonished faces of baby birds, and we see again God's grace, that unmerited, divine favor.

It is true, as well, that we are tempted to inflame a situation, to worsen a wound, by reading into it all sorts of ill. "He said this, I know he meant such-and-such, he hates me, I know . . ." When all we have are facts to go on, it doesn't help to imbue those facts with extra emotions and hidden meaning. What do we know to be true—about God, about this world, about our heart, about a diagnosis or situation? We then leave the rest up to God. (It helps to try to establish better communication patterns, however, so we aren't left wondering about someone's hidden meaning or agenda!)

Rather than becoming mired in present problems, we can learn to look toward the future. "Our present sufferings are not worth comparing with the glory that will be revealed in us," wrote Paul (Romans 8:18). That God has great good in store for us, and glory to show through us, boggles my mind—and trains my eye to look in the right direction.

One woman, with inoperable cancer, heard over and over, "You're dying of cancer." She began correcting them, vibrantly, "No, I'm *living* with cancer." Learning to focus in the midst of the desert brings life.

HOW TO FOCUS

Pray. Philippians 4:6-7 says, "Do not be anxious about anything, but in everything, by prayer and petition, with thanksgiving, present your requests to God. And the peace of God, which transcends all understanding, will guard your hearts and your minds in Christ Jesus."

Paul likely knew what he was talking about since he wrote Philippians from a prison cell. Prayer and petition free us from our problems—they don't eradicate our problems—and result in peace. When Christ's presence stands guard over our mind and heart, the desert cannot imprison us.

Slow down. At a retreat, a dear widow said in her German accent, "It is dangerous to live so busy. You never have time to look inside, to see your soul. You run from one thing to another and you never go deep. You live a shallow life." It's like having attention deficit disorder: we are never able to focus. Limiting our options helps us pay attention.

Let Scripture in. God's word infuses mind and heart, squeezing out compulsive thoughts, doubts, anxieties. A man in recovery from a homosexual lifestyle told me that when old thoughts and habits tempted, he focused his mind on Scripture, on truth. "I took each obsessive thought, wrote it on a three-by-five card and, on the back, wrote a verse from the Bible to combat the lies in my head. Gradually, God's Word became louder and truer to me than the voice in my mind."

Journal. Journaling as a focusing agent helps us still the chaos of emotional firing, the panic of all the what-ifs, and it becomes a receptacle for our emotions. It connects us again with our heart and longings, which are the last things we may notice. Journaling lets us debrief events, ask ourself questions like, "Where does it hurt? What old messages am I be-

TRAVELOGUE

• *When have you*

experienced success in focusing on

God, on what you know to be true

about him, on facts?

• *Which tools are most effective in*

shifting your focus?

lieving right now? What is God asking of me?"

Turn pain into an offering to God. This seems backward, somehow. We want God to take it away from us; how is an affliction an offering? We submit in our heart with a willingness to have this pain shape us and bring God glory. An offering involves giving our life to God, which would include any pain we endure. Like a tithe, or a talent, God can take pain and use it for good in his economy in this world. We give it as a sacrifice.

Before it can become an offering, however, we have to quit rationalizing pain and its counterparts, like anger, quit minimizing, quit ignoring. David Viscott writes:

> When you hold anger inside, you try to reason your pain away— not a good plan, for the mind is designed to feel. You need to feel pain before you can accept it. Accepting pain means putting what you have felt into perspective, a function of reason. However, if you place your pain in perspective too quickly, saying, "Everything works out for the best," when it clearly has not, some pain is excluded from being felt and still needs to be mourned. So the mind has the power both to heal you and prolong your suffering. Until you feel your pain, the mind can grant only limited relief.

CHOOSING GRACE

Choosing to focus in the midst of the chaos will not end our desert sojourn. "Jesus refused to relieve the people's anxieties about the Roman issue, the tax issue, or the issues of health, hunger or religion. Instead, he invited people further into their fears. It was the only way they could find a savior."

In the obscurity of the wilderness, when our heart must have a focal point, we choose Grace. And find a Savior.

Wilderness Response

ACCOMPANIMENT PSALM

We have heard with our ears, O God;
   our fathers have told us
what you did in their days,
   in days long ago.
With your hand you drove out the nations
   and planted our fathers;
you crushed the peoples
   and made our fathers flourish.
It was not by their sword that they won the land,
   nor did their arm bring them victory;
it was your right hand, your arm,
   and the light of your face, for you loved them.
PSALM 44:1-3

DESERT READING

Now faith is being sure of what we hope for and certain of what we do not see. . . .

By faith Moses' parents hid him for three months after he was born, because they saw he was no ordinary child, and they were not afraid of the king's edict.

By faith Moses, when he had grown up, refused to be known as the son of Pharaoh's daughter. He chose to be mistreated along with the people of God rather than to enjoy the pleasures of sin for a short time. He regarded disgrace for the sake of Christ as of greater value than the treasures of Egypt, because he was looking ahead to his reward. By faith he left Egypt, not fearing the king's

anger; he persevered because he saw him who is invisible.
HEBREWS 11:1, 23-26

GUIDING SONG

May the Mind of Christ My Savior

May the mind of Christ my Savior
Live in me from day to day,
By His love and power controlling,
All I do and say.

May the Word of God dwell richly
In my heart from hour to hour,
So that all may see I triumph
Only thru' His power.

May I run the race before me,
Strong and brave to face the foe,
Looking only unto Jesus
As I onward go.

May His beauty rest upon me
As I seek the lost to win,
And may they forget the channel,
Seeing only Him.
WORDS: A. CYRIL BARHAM-GOULD
MUSIC: KATE B. WILKINSON

REMEMBER YOUR JOURNEY

- In solitude, picture your wilderness, your transition. Ask God
  for his viewpoint, his heart and presence.

Still Point

If we had a keen vision and feeling of all ordinary human life,

it would be like hearing the grass grow and the squirrel's heart beat,

and we should die of that roar which lies

on the other side of silence.

GEORGE ELIOT

8

....

CHOOSING TO FEAST

The LORD longs to be gracious to you,

And therefore He waits on high to have compassion on you.

For the LORD is a God of justice;

How blessed are all those who long for Him.

ISAIAH 30:18 NASB

A writing deadline pressed against me. In a scheduling vise, food loses its appeal. Often I work past hunger pains, forgetting to eat. Living too long like this means living on drivenness and fear. Ignoring a natural need means I am not trusting God.

This driven state shutters my eyes from the emeralds sparkling on dew-wet grass, the electric ball of sun teetering on the horizon, the endless blue of sky stretching overhead, the breath of a bird chirping in crisp morning air. Instead, I inhabit a sensory-deprived country.

Deadline looming, I scavenged space at a seminary and began harvesting words. A bell tolled somewhere, and like Pavlov's dog I recognized hunger. Bell = Food. I hurried to the dining hall, not noticing the sky, the birds, the water ahead of the river of students—totally on task. Eat and read, work, work, work.

In line, I grabbed tray, utensils, plate, reached for the first serving spoon. As if a veil lifted, I saw the buffet. Vibrant salad greens, layers of sliced meat, a beautiful array of fresh fruit, hot bread, pepper steak, desserts . . . I blinked at the brilliant colors and lavish display, as though released from a dark prison into bright sun. A still life of Psalm 23: "Thou preparest a table before me in the presence of mine enemies" (KJV).

And I was the enemy, forcing myself away from the natural and normal need for sustenance. But still God provided me with a lush table laden with beauty—and whispered, "Listen to the state of your soul. Your hunger and deprivation are portraits of your heart. Come to me with your hunger."

Hunger is holy. And like an Italian mother, God waves me over, "Eat, eat. You are too skinny. You must eat." I take, and eat, and am filled with the presence of God.

FEASTING AND THE ISRAELITES

What do we learn from our fleeing friends about feasting in times of transition? God said to Moses, "Tell Pharaoh to release you so you can go celebrate a feast to me in the wilderness." A month into their trek, fear ate holes in their faith, their adrenaline rush evaporated and the Passover feast was a gaunt memory.

How easy to mistake the growling of our heart for the rumbling of our tummy. We confuse our hungers. Their thoughts turned to their stomach: "If only we had died by the LORD's hand in Egypt! There we sat around pots of meat and ate all the food we wanted, but you have brought us out into this desert to starve this entire assembly to death" (Exodus 16:3). God responded with grace—the Rescuer continues to deliver from slavery, first to Egypt and then to their appetites. In Moses' words, "In the evening you will know that it was the LORD who brought you out of Egypt, and in the morning you will see the glory of the LORD, because he has heard your grumbling against him" (Exodus 16:6-7). In the gauntness of transition it is easy to mistake God's good intentions toward us.

Even in their complaining against him, God satisfied their hunger, intending that their hunger turn their thoughts to him, to his glory and provision. As if he says, "Bring your hunger to me. I will nourish you."

TRAVELOGUE

• *When do you notice hunger?*

• *What do you do about it, how do you divert it?*

When desire raises its head, whether for food or some other form of "comfort," God waits to comfort us—not to shut down our hungers, our longings, but to redirect them. This is not a God of slavery who feeds our stomach but keeps our heart in bondage. This is the God to whom we turn when we are fed, and we give glory.

FEAST ON GOD

Old Testament feasts centered around food and festivities—but they were not about food. They were designed to bring the Israelites' heart back to the Lord their God, to his provisions and protection. Christ refers to himself as the "bread of life" (John 6:35), of which the manna in the wilderness was a type. He tells us, "Just as the living Father sent me and I live because of the Father, so the one who feeds on me will live because of me. This is the bread that came down from heaven. Our forefathers ate manna and died, but he who feeds on this bread will live forever" (John 6:57-58).

Food—hunger—is the common language of humanity. Hunger opens our heart to God's presence and power, creating room for God to act. Deuteronomy 8:3 (NASB) says, "He humbled you, and let you be hungry, and fed you with manna which you did not know, that He might make you understand that man does not live by bread alone, but man lives by everything that proceeds out of the mouth of the LORD."

In Exodus 5:1 (NASB) "the LORD, the God of Israel," says, "Let My people go that they may celebrate a feast to Me in the wilderness." The wilderness is perfect for feasting on God because our enslaving distractions become obvious or are removed. Hunger is good. Hunger is holy. And if we are listening deeply to the external surface hungers and their internal, eternal drive, our longings will lead us to God.

"Longing is the heart's treasury," wrote Augustine:

> Give me a man in love, he knows what I mean. Give me one who yearns; give me one who is hungry; give me one far away in this desert, who is thirsty and sighs for the spring of the Eternal Country. . . . But if I speak to a cold man, he just doesn't know what I am talking about.

Hunger is also a kindness. *The Cloud of Unknowing* says:

> At one time you were caught up in the *Common* manner of the Christian life in a day-to-day mundane existence along with your friends. But I think that the eternal love of God, which had once created you out of nothing and then redeemed you from Adam's curse through the sacrifice of his blood, could not bear to let you go on living so common a life far from him. And so, with exquisite kindness, he awakened desire within you, and binding it fast with the leash of love's longing, drew you closer to himself.

The desert is vital—it awakens our thirst and our hunger—if we have tuned our heart to hear the voice of our Lover, beckoning us, drawing us to him through these longings.

Unfortunately, we just aren't always listening.

Job said, "My gauntness rises up and testifies against me" (Job 16:8), and now, thousands of years later, we are the most overly resourced religious community in the world—and the most emaciated of spirit. We starve ourselves to death spiritually, feeding our hungry heart with food, activity, indulgence, work, substances—none of which satisfy the ache in our soul. Isaiah asks, "Why spend money on what is not bread, and your labor on what does not satisfy? Listen, listen to me, and eat what is good, and your soul will delight in the richest of fare" (Isaiah 55:22).

For years I wanted to blame my husband, my church, my upbringing, my children, anyone who ventured near, for my soul emaciation. A transition, a time of brokenness when I recognized my own desperation for something beyond the visible and beyond my own extremely finite wisdom, propelled me beyond the "sue someone—blame others" mentality, like the man who sued the fast food giants because he gained weight eating there. A growth surge began when I stopped making excuses and began to deliberately feed on Scripture, prayer, contemplative reading, even beauty. These disciplines nurture us in times of transition. Writes Dorothy Bass:

> Though the repetition can lull us into boredom or complacency, there is no other way. The days we embrace in this practice [of receiving the day] are like manna: they cannot be hoarded. When the day brings suffering, enduring this day's suffering, not dreading next month's deterioration, is the necessity of this day. When the day brings testing or opportunity, to meet this free from bondage to the past or dread of the future is the day's urgency. Jesus taught his disciples to ask God for bread for this day, not for all of them.

If we trust God's heart toward us enough, we will come to him for each day's sustenance.

FEAST WITH SUBSTANCE

Experts in survival teach appropriate eating patterns for the wilderness: drink water, not pop or alcohol; given a choice of food or water, drink water because food requires so much water for digestion and assimilation that eating can actually dehydrate us. Poor planners in the desert are frequently found delirious, sunburned, lost. Or dead.

In our wilderness of transition, nourishing our soul goes against our nature in crisis or change; even routine spiritual self-care is easily neglected as panic or push mode takes over.

At the diagnosis of prostate cancer, Gretchen and David's desert strategy was not to literally fast, but to fill. They read classics on suffering, mercy and grace, and tanked up on Scripture. They prayed and praised and openly shared their heart with close friends. They changed their diets, together, eating natural foods, eliminating excess, strengthening one another for surgery and recovery.

These friends also deliberately fortified their relationship, pondering the what-ifs—risks and potential problems—and committing to their love for one another regardless of outcome.

In the desert, hunger is deadly; they knew they needed to feast together to sustain them through a long, lean wilderness march. "Get up and eat, for the journey is too much for you," the angel of the Lord told Elijah before his long run through the desert (1 Kings 19:7).

FEAST WITH SINGING

Rich and I sneaked away before launching into this place of abandonment, this itinerant calling, relinquishing security in the form of regular paychecks, a business car, health insurance, pension, housing allowance and reimbursed business expenses. Questions ate at us: how would we survive, how would we trust God, feed our family, pay our bills? Sensing the desert's hot breath of change approaching, we sang from the hymnal en route—every song we could find on God's guidance, provisions, protection. From "Be Thou My Vision" to "Guide Me, O Thou Great Jehovah," from "Where He Leads Me" to "Savior Like a Shepherd Lead Us," our mouths formed the words while our hearts slowly embraced them. God would guide us.

We returned without definite answers. But the gentle practice of singing, of aligning our hearts with God's truth through the great hymns, fed our souls and chastened our fear about leaving the local pastorate for a broader, riskier place of ministry.

FEAST WITH BEAUTY

Yesterday, at a college visitation with my daughter, we climbed to the tenth floor. I had just wrangled and shouted at a parking lot attendant, who swore at me because of my ugliness. Shame ate away at me even as I listened to the tour guide and speakers.

The school faces Lake Michigan, and picture windows offer panoramic views. The aqua beauty transfixed me, feeding a long-neglected part of my soul. Blue water, waves, glowing sun—all identified and fed a hunger in my heart, emptiness that had displayed itself in the parking lot. Nature, beauty—all are God's invitation, the crooking of his finger, beckoning us to come, taste and see that the Lord is good.

FEAST WITH FASTING

One winter, I chain-read short secular romances. Like a smoker lights the next cigarette from the burning tip of the previous one, I finished a book and set it down with one hand, picking up the next one with my other hand. Weeks before Easter, after an entire season of this addiction, I was convicted. My kids were tired of vying for my attention, my husband wondered when I would come back from this alternate existence, and God longed for my heart. I gave up fiction for six weeks, and read Scripture and contemplative writing.

With a crucial board meeting approaching, a friend of mine felt impressed by God to fast. The biggest benefit was the focusing effect of going without food: focusing on God, on the state of her heart, on the quality of her words. In that withdrawal period, the Lord redirected her longing for comfort from food to the bread of life.

In the desert, a practical means of fasting is resting. We rest by refusing to work. We rest as we refuse to indulge in panic or shouting. We rest by saving up the energy required by movement.

Health conditions prevent many from literal fasting. Fasting from work—resting instead of trying to save ourself with frantic effort—is a life-saving desert technique. Eugene Peterson says, "When I quit my

TRAVELOGUE

• *When do you find*

yourself compulsively feeding,

whether on substances,

relationships, activities? Certain

times of day? Where?

• *When you realize you are heading*

for the fridge, or the computer, or

the television, or the phone, or the

mall, stop yourself. Stay in your

desire, your restlessness, but invite

God into it with you. Ask him to

show you the deepest desire of your

heart and to come and fill that

desire. Rather than feeding

yourself with something that will

not satisfy, let our Lord feed you

with the bread of heaven.

day's work, nothing essential stops. I go to sleep to get out of the way for a while. I get into the rhythm of salvation. . . . Human effort is honored and respected not as a thing in itself but by its integration into the rhythms of grace and blessing."

We might consider ceasing our all-consuming work patterns to allow God some freedom to do his thing in our life. In working endlessly, we begin to think that all our being, all our income, all our accomplishments, are due to our hard work. We pride ourselves on working hard; America applauds while our families fall apart, our faith disintegrates and our health crumbles.

In the desert, the better part of faith is resting. However we fast, whether from food to eternal food, from work to rest, or from words to silence, the Lord of the wilderness says, in Psalm 46:10, "Cease striving and know that I am God" (NASB).

MISPLACED FEASTING: THE BATTLE FOR OUR HEART

Learning to feast is integral to recognizing and honoring our deepest longings. But the battle is not yet over. There's a turf war to derail our heart. A friend complained that household items kept disappearing. A visit to the vet for her ailing basset hound yielded the missing spoon, a ring, underwear, a dish towel, some marbles. On what are we feeding? Why do we consume that which does not allay our hunger, which will never satisfy?

Maybe we just don't recognize hunger, don't think about feasting because we've subverted or ignored our hunger for so long. A deadened heart ceases to dream, to hunger, to long. But the answer is not, "I'm not hungry." Oh, we are hungry. We are one step away from death in the desert. We are famished but pay no attention to our true hunger. Simone Weil says, "The danger is that the soul should persuade itself that it is not hungry. It can only persuade itself of this by lying."

We do this because we live in a battle zone. This is warfare territory, with a very real enemy who wants to use our God-given longings for evil. Satan knows that a heart feeding on junk will never thrive, knows that if he can divert our deepest longing for enduring, unconditional love then he wins the battle for our heart. Remember the Israelites: "In the desert they gave in to their craving" (Psalm 106:14)?

While we feed on rocks like the basset hound, the enemy, the author of all lies, especially lies that pertain to our heart, gleefully imagines our desert demise. Hunger is his weapon, like the Mogadishu warlord in *Black Hawk Down* who used hunger to keep his people in submission. Satan tells us, "Do not listen to your hunger." Or he mocks us with, "You are not hungry for God. You need food, activity, substances, power or people." "Emptiness," writes Calvin Miller, "leaves us wanton till we fill it with whatever secondary appetite might seem to stop our hungers of the soul."

When Jesus visited the desert, without food for forty days, Satan wanted to use Jesus' hunger for evil. "I'll make these stones into bread," the enemy wheedled, "if you'll just . . ." But notice that Jesus didn't say, "OK, I won't hunger then, because hunger is dangerous." No, Jesus used hunger appropriately. His hunger forced his attention and reliance onto

God; he refused to assuage the pain with anything other than God's presence and turned instead to God's word for sustenance. His response: "Man does not live on bread alone, but on every word that comes from the mouth of God" (Matthew 4:4). It's a lie that desires are improper, selfish. What's improper or selfish is how we sometimes choose to fulfill these desires. If we let our desires be diverted from God's heart, the purpose of desire will be sabotaged.

And God is faithful; he pledges food in the wilderness of our longings. "You give them to drink of the river of Your delights" (Psalm 36:8 NASB). "You still the hunger of those you cherish" (Psalm 17:14). Isaiah 49:9-11 promises:

> They will feed beside the roads
>> and find pasture on every barren hill.
> They will neither hunger nor thirst,
>> nor will the desert heat or the sun beat upon them.
> He who has compassion on them will guide them
>> and lead them beside springs of water.

Just as he did with Jesus, though, Satan loves to play on our hungers for love, power, food, security. We cannot allow him the upper hand. Unless we recognize our hungers they will hijack us spiritually and starve us. The enemy of our soul waits to redirect our hunger—for God, for love that endures—onto other false gods. Or numbness.

If our heart has ceased its longings, fossilizing in the heat of the desert, what do we do? Perhaps our heart lies behind us like a tattered, useless, empty rucksack. We must return to where we left our heart abandoned along the trail.

If you do not hunger, ask God to take you back to where you lost your heart. We need to renew the search and rescue for our lost or sabotaged hunger, our desires, our dreams. Recovering our heart requires pain as we revisit old wounds, give them to God, grieve and release the perpetrators and the pain, receiving the Comforter's presence, hope and love in that place of brokenness.

We must bring our appetites, and our extinguished longings, to God. What does he want to do with our hunger? Always, always he wants to be the source of our nurturance, as our provider, our "Chef." As the Giver of all good gifts—and hunger is a good gift— in him our hunger will be appeased. Thomas Merton prayed:

> Lord, Give me a hunger for
> yourself
> That cannot be sated by
> Any other human thing.

In this place of in-between and transition, this deserted, desert place, we cannot let the enemy distract us from our true desire or douse our true desire with deadness, with not wanting. May God

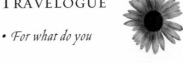

TRAVELOGUE

• *For what do you yearn? What are the longings of your heart, how have you numbed them?*

• *When have you cried out of longing for something, someone? What or who was it, and did you feel shame for that desire or those tears? Could you allow God to receive all your desires and fulfill them with his love?*

sharpen our hunger for him, that all discontent would be directed toward him, that he might awaken our deepest, truest longings.

Hunger, in the wilderness, becomes an intersection, a grace point, with the Lover of our soul and his total acceptance. In him we find our deepest hungers fulfilled.

Wilderness Response

ACCOMPANIMENT PSALM

They wandered in the wilderness in a desert region. . . .
They were hungry and thirsty;
Their soul fainted within them.
They cried out to the LORD in their trouble;
He delivered them out of their distresses. . . .
Let them give thanks to the LORD for His lovingkindness. . . .
For He has satisfied the thirsty soul,
And the hungry soul He has filled with what is good.
PSALM 107:4-9 NASB

DESERT READING

Moreover, I will give you a new heart and put a new spirit within
you; and I will remove the heart of stone from your flesh and give
you a heart of flesh. I will put My Spirit within you and cause you
to walk in My statutes, and you will be careful to observe My or-
dinances. You will live in the land that I gave to your forefathers;
so you will be My people, and I will be your God. Moreover . . .
I will call for the grain and multiply it, and I will not bring a fam-
ine on you. I will multiply the fruit of the tree and the produce of
the field, that you may not receive again the disgrace of famine
among the nations.
EZEKIEL 36:26-30 NASB

GUIDING SONG

Jesus I Am Resting, Resting
Jesus I am resting, resting

In the joy of what Thou art;
I am finding out the greatness
Of Thy loving heart.
Thou hast bid my gaze upon Thee
And Thy beauty fills my soul,
For by Thy transforming power
Thou hast made me whole.

Simply trusting Thee, Lord Jesus,
I behold Thee as Thou art.
And Thy love so pure, so changeless,
Satisfies my heart.
Satisfies its deepest longings,
Meets, supplies its every need,
And surrounds me with its blessings;
Thine is love indeed!

AUTHOR UNKNOWN

REMEMBER YOUR JOURNEY

- How will you let yourself feast in the wilderness? What would prohibit you from such soul sustenance? Can you trust God enough to give him your deepest longings and let him nurture you?

Still Point

Stillness is the precondition of presence.

I must first be still to myself if I am to be still with another.

DAVID BENNER

9

....

CHOOSING SPIRITUAL FRIENDSHIP

And I will pour out . . . a spirit of grace and supplication.

ZECHARIAH 12:10

*T*he phone rang in the middle of Luann's busy day. As God would have it, she was between meetings and the call came straight to her. "Luann," her friend whispered, tears tightening her voice, "I don't know what to do about my son. He is using drugs."

Luann delayed her next appointment and listened. She asked wise questions. She shared ideas when appropriate. And she prayed over the phone. Luann's total availability and her own grief as she wept with her friend gave hope and direction—and much needed companionship in the often overwhelming wasteland of transition.

There is no greater privilege than being present to another person in pain. No greater gift in desert times than to know we do not traverse the barren plains alone. No greater joy than holding another in time of crisis, carrying that person to the Father and, with love, transferring our loved one to him. Much like cradling a child and then passing the child into her parent's arms, so a good friend holds us and carries us to our Abba, our Daddy. How God longs to love us through relationships with others.

WILDERNESS FRIENDSHIP

When God summoned Moses back from his forty-year escape tending sheep, Moses' final protest was, "Look, God, I know all about you, but, hey, I just need someone else to do this." When he'd run out of other reasons, Moses said, "You know I can't talk well so just send someone else, OK?"

God's anger showed up then: "What about your brother, Aaron the Levite? I know he can speak well. He is already on his way to meet you, and his heart will be glad when he sees you" (Exodus 4:14). That was miracle enough since there is no record in Scripture of Moses and Aaron meeting since the day baby Moses floated away from his family down the Nile. We don't know if their mother told Aaron and Miriam to "watch out for that Pharaoh's grandson, he's really your brother." But somehow, Aaron found Moses and approached him—as a brother. And even though he had plenty of reasons to be furious with Moses for disappearing and abandoning his strategic position within the king's empire, Aaron's "heart was glad" when he saw Moses.

And from two estranged brothers raised in entirely different households, one a slave and pauper, another a once-wealthy prince, God created a wilderness team that would endure forty years. "You shall speak to him and put words in his mouth; I will help both of you speak and will teach you what to do. He will speak to the people for you, and it will be as if he were your mouth and as if you were God to him" (Exodus 4:15-17).

Rarely can we survive the wilderness alone, though this is our proclivity. Rarely are we intended to do so. Thankfully, the God who created us knows our need for companionship and accountability, in spite of our protests. He formed a desert partnership that would rescue a nation from slavery, take them on a four-decade journey of faith and save them. He longs to create desert partnerships for us, as well. As with Moses and Aaron, spiritual friendships complete our weaknesses.

I hesitate to use the word *fellowship* here. Although the essence of real fellowship is one starving person showing another where to find bread, the term itself conjures up images of potlucks and red Jell-O in dank church basements, of flighty conversation and "I'm fine-ness" in the foyer and aisles of church. Perhaps less trivialized is the term *spiritual friendship*. A primary understanding of a spiritual friend, according to David Benner in *Sacred Companions*,

> is that the deep knowing of both self and God foundational to Christian spirituality demands deep knowing of and being known by others. Neither knowing God nor knowing self can progress very far apart from others who are able and willing to offer us help. . . . Intimate relationships with others prepare us for intimacy with God. . . . The gift of those who accompany us on the spiritual journey is [that] . . . they help us become people who are capable of intimacy. The transforming work of becoming the great lovers that Christ desires us to be demands the grist of more intimate relationships.

A SPIRITUAL FRIEND

Spiritual friendships begin with companionship. Rather than trying to teach us, a desert friend comes alongside us in our sojourn. This sense of equality, of traveling in the same direction side by side, feeling the same anguish en route, is essential for true mutuality. Though our journeys through fire may differ, traveling together creates strength.

I will never forget the treasured times deepening friends have said, "I would like to tell you more of my story." So often we withhold our history because we are afraid another will judge us, ignore our painful past, or shy away from acknowledging the ugliness and anguish there.

Further, a true friend sees a spark within us and blows it into flame, beckoning our strengths and gifts. C. S. Lewis asked:

> Are not all life long friendships born at that moment when at last you meet another human being who has some inkling (but faint and uncertain even in the best) of that something which you were

born desiring, and which, beneath the louder passions, night and day, year by year, from childhood to old age, you are looking for, watching for, listening for?

These friends look further than our superficialities and incomes and soapboxes and cleverly applied makeup and flighty talk and well-decorated homes (or the lack thereof, in my case). Spiritual friends fight for us: fight for us to become the person God intended all along, reminding us where we are going. They see who we will be, not necessarily who we are now. "To truly love someone is to see them as God intended," said Fyodor Dostoyevsky.

How wonderful to hear, "I'm in this with you for the long haul." A spiritual friend shows us more about God by loving us well, with an intention to "do us good." This intentionality creates safety and longevity, freeing us to transition wholly, provided we stay focused on God and his purposes for each of us. To do this we must remain open, stay honest and be available.

Intense listening is one of God's traits and a characteristic of a dear friend. We've all had—or been—acquaintances who did all the talking and none of the listening when we were together; we never offer one another the chance to be part of the relationship. Monologues prohibit true friendship. Dietrich Bonhoeffer wrote:

> It is God's love for us that he not only gives us his Word but also lends us his ear. So it is his work that we do for our brother when we learn to listen to him. Christians, especially preachers, so often think they must always "contribute" something when they are in the company of others, that this is the one service they have to render. They forget that listening can be a greater service than speaking.

We carry this thinking into the wilderness as well: we must always be contributing something, always be the one offering consolation and service. Listening—hushing our anxious heart and listening to God, to others, to our own clamoring—becomes a primary task and tool of the wilderness, as does humbly allowing another into that place of silence, where they can love us.

A spiritual friend invites enlargement—"Tell me more about that"; "What was that like for you?"—and is not afraid to ask difficult questions: "What was happening for you there?" "How do you feel about that?" "What did you mean by . . . ?" "Can I ask you about . . . ?"

DESERT DIFFICULTIES

Knowing we were created for meaningful, completing relationships from the very beginning of time does not eliminate the difficulties inherent in finding those friends and sustaining them in our world today. Several factors mitigate against soul-level friendships.

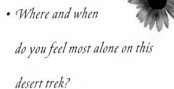

TRAVELOGUE

• *Where and when do you feel most alone on this desert trek?*

• *When have wilderness friends carried you to God? What happened? How did that make you feel about yourself? God?*

• *For which of these characteristics do you most long in a friend? When has a friend exhibited such gifts in your life?*

"Attachment disorder" and relationship needs. Several friends of mine have adopted children. Their dearly loved and much wanted children have reactive attachment disorder (RAD), likely based in some sense of early abandonment, so they repel love though it is their heart's desire.

What a picture of our heart as well. We fight against the very thing for which we most long. This shows up in our chock-full calendars, our harried conversations and shallow relationships; both society and lifestyle collaborate against trust, depth and longevity. Friends take time.

They require freedom, spontaneity, courage. They are not efficient and will wreck our carefully programmed pocket calendars. We have to choose, deliberately, to listen to our good longings and refuse to stay in cahoots with the isolation of the enemy any longer. We cannot afford to live friendless.

Transience. Our transient society makes it harder to dive below the surface with others and stay there longer and longer. One Chicago suburb has an average residency rate of eighteen months! It's easy, then, to just say, "Forget it, I'm not going to risk, to invest; I won't be here that long." But, the more profound our friendships, the more mutual our sharing, the easier it is to maintain relationships even at a distance. God has planted dear friends for me across North America. When we connect, we don't have to catch up on full details of life but on our hearts. In one minute on the phone we've plumbed the depths.

Nurturing as control. Receiving love somehow obligates us, thus we have to give up some measure of control in order to receive. Some people refuse to be in that vulnerable, I-owe-you position and so do not allow themselves to accept nurture from others.

Fear of rejection. Perhaps one of our greatest wilderness wrestlings is with our sense of worth. "Am I enough?" we ask. We question whether we deserve (need) healthy, deeply supportive relationships and whether we have something to offer in return. "Is there enough beauty and life within me to sustain and deepen a friendship?" Inside us dwells a classic fear of being rejected if anyone really knew the depth of our internal depravity, how dark it gets inside us at times. Merton writes:

> To love sincerely, and with simplicity, we must first of all overcome
> the fear of not being loved. And this cannot be done by forcing
> ourselves to believe in some illusion, saying that we are loved
> when we are not. We must first strip ourselves of our greatest illu-
> sions about ourselves, frankly recognize in how many ways we are
> unlovable, descend into the depths of our being until we come to

the basic reality that is in us, and learn to see that we are loveable after all, in spite of everything!

What a miracle: in spite of us, God loves us. Because of that unending grace, we can engage in spiritual friendships—without fear. This helps when we fear offending another with our honesty, our past, our besetting sins, the pain we have endured.

Past training. One friend always had to be happy, never having any problems, doubts or pain as a child. Now she is trying to undo age-old patterns. She wrote me, after identifying a need for support, "I thought I would ask you to lift me up in prayer. I am so used to doing my life alone, and I think it would be really good for me to let someone be with me a little in this." How logical that we would try to go it alone in general, and particularly in times of transition. After all, it is in relationships where we are wounded. Douglas Webster agrees:

> The preeminent source of pain in this culture is broken relation-ships. The only war many people experience firsthand is the war going on inside their homes and within themselves. This is the war that rages between husband and wife, parents and children, and soul and spirit. This is where we feel the spiritual famine, the emo-tional drought and the physical pain. It is in our friendships, our marriages, our families and in our very selves that we feel this lean-ness of soul—this humiliation.

Because of our primary relationship with the God who will never leave us or forsake us (Hebrews 13:5), we can also spread out from him into relationships where we dare to trust again, cooperating with the longings he has sown into our soul.

KNOWING

In order to be known, we must, as Benner suggested, be willing to know ourself, first. Acknowledging our ache for what it is, loneliness, is a first step. Nouwen writes:

Here [in the monastery] I have the chance to convert my feelings of loneliness into solitude and allow God to enter into the emptiness of my heart. Here I can experience a little bit of the desert and realize that it is not only a dry place where people die of thirst but also the vast empty space where the God of love reveals himself and offers his promise to those who are waiting in faithfulness.

TRAVELOGUE

- *What holds you back from spiritual friendships? What excuses do you make? Where do you hide?*

- *How does your family of origin contribute to the way you "do" friendship?*

- *How do you react to isolation? When have you allowed it to become a spiritual tool, shaping you?*

In this place of acknowledgment, we are set free. When God camps in the midst of our loneliness, the desert begins its transforming work. We can give our longings to God, and even as we search the horizon ourselves, allow him to begin to bring us the people at the right time who will wait out our wilderness with us. Then the desert loses its sterility and becomes alive and meaningful. As Ronald Wilson writes, "Small pleasures and deep satisfactions, as well as doubts, failures, and temptations, find meaning in community."

A REAL FRIEND

With a real friend, I don't have to be Fine. I don't have to be someone with all the answers and none of the problems of life. I can be a wreck. My heart can ache, and I can say, "I am not doing well. I want to quit. This is just too hard." I am humbled by the number of friends who can hold me in my messiness, not feeling obliged to run the other way or to fix me up.

Nor do they judge my wreckage; I do not believe there is anything I could do to run them off—not my deepest secret or my darkest shame. These women need no performance; I don't need to entertain or wow them with compelling and meaningful talk (good thing). I don't need to impress them with my mind or change their minds or convince them of anything about myself. I can just be there with them.

I come away from spiritual friends challenged, longing to be more like Christ, to be a better woman, a present and alive wife, a loving mother, a steady friend—and to make a difference in the world. Chesterton was right: "There are no words to express the abyss between isolation and having one ally. It may be conceded to the mathematician that four is twice two. But two is not twice one; two is two thousand times one."

With spiritual friends, there is no poverty in the wilderness. These companions, like the Magi, bring us to Christ with the gift of their friendship.

My friends will not allow me to give up on God, on myself, on those I love or my place in their life. Like a mother taking her daughter's chin in her hands and saying, "Look at me. Look into my eyes," so friends hold my heart and redirect my attention: to God's good heart for me, to the goodness of my longings (rather than the way those longings are displayed—the messiness). They adjure me to hold on. And when I cannot hold on, they hold on for me. In my place.

THE TEMPTATION

A challenge of friendship is that we never allow our earthly relationships, regardless of how perfect, how dear, how deep, how transparent, how beckoning they are, we never allow them to replace or supplant our relationship with God. Consider Exodus 4:17, the tail end of the story of Moses and Aaron meeting and completing one another. God set up this dynamic duo for desert drama, and even while glorying in that combi-

TRAVELOGUE

• Who was the first

friend who looked past all your

externals and into the very heart

of who God created you to be?

What was that like for you?

• When has a friend held on to you

when you could not hold on for

yourself?

• When are you most tempted to

run to friends instead of to God?

How do you combat that

tendency?

nation, he adds, "But take this staff in your hand so you can perform miraculous signs with it."

We are never to forget that it is God who works the miraculous. Friends are miraculous, and it is the Lord of the Exodus, the master of our transitions, who weaves lives together in the wilderness. He is the One who will accomplish all that concerns us. How easy to run first with our pain and problems to our spiritual friends, rather than lifting our eyes to God and screaming, "Oh, help, help. I cannot do this alone." The Lord says, "Take the staff"—his staff—so that we will never release our grasp on God and his glory and might.

THE GLORY OF FRIENDSHIP

No wonder George Eliot said, "Friendship . . . my wellspring in the wilderness." Real friendships turn our wilderness into worship.

The LORD said to Aaron, "Go into the desert to meet Moses." So he met Moses at the mountain of God and kissed him. Then Moses told Aaron everything the LORD had sent him to say, and also about all the miraculous signs he had commanded him to perform.

Moses and Aaron brought together all the elders of the Israelites, and Aaron told them everything the LORD had said to Moses. He also performed the signs before the people, and they believed. And when they heard that the LORD was concerned about them and had seen their misery, they bowed down and worshiped. (Exodus 4:27-31)

Together they were stronger than when apart. Together they completed one another's weaknesses. Together their impact on millions of people—billions, considering that Christ's coming depended on their deliverance from slavery in Egypt, which brings us all the way from Moses' time to today—moves me to worship. Surely this same God is the Lord of our Desert. Surely this God will bring us into places of spiritual friendship.

And our wilderness friendships, forged in the wounds and weariness of the world, will transform the desert for others as well. And together we will bow down and worship. Together we will choose grace in the wilderness.

The Wilderness Response

ACCOMPANIMENT PROVERB

A friend loves at all times. . . .

Perfume and incense bring joy to the heart,
and the pleasantness of one's friend springs from his earnest counsel.

Do not forsake your friend and the friend of your father,
and do not go to your brother's house when adversity strikes—
better a neighbor who is nearby
than a brother far away.

PROVERBS 17:17; 27:9-10

DESERT READING

David . . . bowed down before Jonathan three times, with his face to the ground. Then they kissed each other and wept together— but David wept the most.

Jonathan said to David, "Go in peace, for we have sworn friendship with each other in the name of the LORD, saying, 'The LORD is witness between you and me, and between your descendants and my descendants forever.'". . . And Saul's son Jonathan went to David . . . and helped him find strength in God.

1 SAMUEL 20:41-42; 23:16

GUIDING SONG

Wonderful Words of Life

Sing them over again to me—
Wonderful words of Life;
Let me more of their beauty see—

Wonderful words of Life.
Words of life and beauty,
Teach me faith and duty . . .

Refrain:
Beautiful words, wonderful words,
Wonderful words of Life;
Beautiful words, wonderful words,
Wonderful words of Life.

Sweetly echo the gospel call—
Wonderful words of Life;
Offer pardon and peace to all—
Wonderful words of Life.
Jesus, only Savior,
Sanctify forever . . .
WORDS AND MUSIC: PHILIP P. BLISS

REMEMBER YOUR JOURNEY

- What is your deepest friendship wound? deepest longing? Pray out those wounds and longings before the Lord now.

Still Point

May the Son of God who is already formed in you grow in you—

so that in you He will become immeasurable,

and that in you He will become laughter,

exultation and the fullness of Joy which no one can take from you.

ISAAC OF STELLA, 1169

10

....

Choosing to Find Fun

We have seen his glory, the glory of the One and Only,
who came from the Father, full of grace and truth.

JOHN 1:14

On a rare trip to a warehouse store, with its towering shelves of over-sized merchandise, I heard laughter ring from one of the aisles. As I rounded the corner, a man in a red jacket stood with a mother and her son, both entranced.

"Why couldn't the bicycle stand up?" he asked. His audience shook their heads, grinning. "It was two tired." Like a wealthy man peeling off bills from his wallet, he rolled out one joke after another in a seemingly endless repertoire of good will.

A fixture at the store, this gentleman likely has other functions in his job description, but by far his most valuable contribution is enhancing the morale of every customer he meets. I have never seen him without multiple jokes to share. He dispenses smiles and leaves joy in his wake.

Who else finds a warehouse store funny? Warehouse stores epitomize transitions, as far as I'm concerned. Stock up—you never know when the end is near. Very desert-like thinking.

I forget about laughter, about fun in the desert. The dust, the heat, the hard work: all combine to keep me from joy.

WATER-PLAY IN THE WILDERNESS

But we have role models for fun in the desert—consider the Israelites. Imagine their thirst, when they were begging God to provide drink in the desert, whining to Moses about their (legitimate) dehydration. They were hot, parched, dirty, cranky and scared. The Lord answered when Moses struck a rock and water gushed out (Exodus 17:1-7). So, like kindergartners, the Israelites stood in an orderly line, single file, and waited their five-second turn at the drinking fountain. A timekeeper stood nearby to enforce timeliness and to prohibit anyone from gulping more than the allotted quantity.

I doubt it. I envision our wilderness companions laughing uproariously, having splash fights like kids in the city when the fire hydrant is opened, jumping in and out of the water, making mud pies, whooping and hollering, filling up their water bottles and emptying them over their friends' heads (the origin of hydrotherapy.) Full, water-enhanced joy!

Even in the dry, dusty, often-discouraging desert of transitions, we have to choose to find fun, somehow, somewhere.

A WHALE OF A DAY

Several years ago, a year into our ministry transition, stress lined my face and filched pounds from my body. I was speaking in New Hampshire and stayed for a few days on Massachusetts' Atlantic coast. Mornings I awakened and scrambled down to the dining room, ready for coffee and God and desperately eager to see the sun rise over the crashing waves and rocks just outside the window.

What one thing would I love to do while there? Just one thing?

I wanted to go whale watching.

The only problem was my terror. The ocean is deep. Deeper than I want to even consider. And whales are big. They could tip the boat over!

(I'd never heard of this happening except for the mechanical shark in *Jaws,* but this still seemed a legitimate possibility.) My husband helpfully recommended whale repellant.

The morning of my voyage, I awoke at 3:00 a.m. to violent weather outside and heaved a sigh of relief: *Oh, good, now I can cancel the trip without cowardice because obviously we can't go out in a tempest.* They'd just finished filming *A Perfect Storm* in that seaside village, so the moral to the story was clear: avoid storms on the ocean at all costs.

By 5:00 a.m. the rain slowed to a fine mist. By 7:00 a.m. a flamboyant sun burned off all remains of inclement weather.

With a mixture of fear and expectancy, I headed off to the Yankee Fleet for my twenty-four dollars worth of dream fulfillment, of an oasis in the desert.

On the boat, the cool ocean breeze blew over me, the day full of just-washed freshness. I watched the waters alertly for looming peril, jerking my life jacket taut. But within, the chant, "God is doing something, God is doing something," heightened my anticipation and shifted my focus. In spite of the naturalist's warning, "Don't get your hopes up. Some of you have seen numerous whales with us. They aren't showing up this summer. But we'll try to find one or two."

But God *was* up to something; the certainty sliced through my fears cleanly. I watched with pure enchantment: the water sprays, the birds. I laughed at whale stats: a whale exhales at 250 miles per hour! This explains the huge spray—visible from long distances across the water—when they blow water through their air hole.

We chased around for a time, searching. Finally, as the ocean reached a particular depth, our oceanographer called over the loudspeaker, "Whale on port" (whichever side that is). We rushed to look. "Whale on starboard . . . " and we heaved to the other side. Soon whales surrounded us. At one point, five whales surfaced, hanging around our boat. Our boat!

"This is most unusual whale behavior," the naturalist said. Whales need to breathe every four to six minutes, so typically they come up for a "blow" and an inhale, then dive again. But these whales—our whales!—slapped their tails and rolled sideways and hung upside down in the water. They turned over and over. Two adolescent whales appeared to be flirting with one another.

"This is extremely rare whale behavior," our guide in khaki repeated, enjoying the show right along with us. "Whales don't perform for humans out here. They are doing this all on their own."

The feeling that God was orchestrating this for us—for me—grew. But even more, I sensed that the whales were simply enjoying God, delighting in their place in the scheme of creation.

In all, we counted nearly twenty whales: eleven humpbacks, seven minke and a small fin whale.

Like a lover, God wooed me with his whale play. In the middle of my desert, the trip on the Yankee Fleet was a breathtaking display of God's creative glee. He showed himself! And he showed me his heart for me. Later that week when I was speaking, a woman in the audience asked, "When have you felt God's love most strongly?"

"On Tuesday," I answered. "When I went on a whale watching trip."

BACK TO REALITY

But honestly, how often do we get to glimpse the ocean in our desert sojourn, much less ride on it and watch for whales? We expect no oasis, not even a mirage. We keep our head down, shield our eyes from the sun and plod forward. Laughter is a stranger, its heart-lifting endorphin far from our experiences. Transitions are somber work, fun is frivolous, and we need to just get going quickly so we can get through, shake the sand off our feet and never look behind.

Right?

Wrong. The dust of the desert is the perfect place to learn to laugh and play again. This is why our children's hospital offers hospital bingo, play areas and computer rooms for kids and teens, with massages for parents. Just into our current ongoing transition of trust, my daughter and I saw

Robin Williams in *Patch Adams*. The movie, and the true story on which it is based, exemplifies laughter and joy as healing elements in lives filled with pain and illness.

Patch spouts to a supervisor, who is unimpressed with Patch's laughter-inducing treatment of patients, "Laughter increases the secretion of endorphins which in turn increases oxygenation of the blood, relaxes the arteries, speeds up the heart, decreases blood pressure, which has a positive effect on all cardiovascular and respiratory ailments as well as overall increasing the immune system response."

TRAVELOGUE

• *When have laughter and fun rescued you from darkness or despondency? Did it feel irreverent to you in a place of mourning?*

• *When, in play, have you felt God's love strongly? In what ways is it hard to give yourself permission to play in the desert?*

The *American Journal of Medicine* concurs with King Solomon: "A cheerful heart is good medicine, but a crushed spirit dries up the bones" (Proverbs 17:22).

In the midst of our soul darkness, I spurted with laughter at Adams's outrageous antics. And now, every time I pull that memory from the bank, I remember the healing time with my firstborn, and I smile all over again.

Fun also breaks down social barriers and eases our grief. After the tragic events of September 11, 2001, comedians closed their mouths in mourning. Sorrow and fear wrapped themselves about our nation like a cloak, and humor felt irreverent. Then, after several months, it became apparent that what our grieving country needed in the wilderness was laughter. The funny people started laughing again, plucking us out of the vacuum of tragedy and into a place of healing.

SOBER CHRISTIANS

Similar to the medical profession displayed in *Patch Adams,* perhaps there is also a serious misunderstanding of Christianity, both inside and outside its ranks. How many times have opponents said, "Christians don't have any fun"? Hilarity is rare unless you're part of a crazy youth group. After that, grow up fast and get serious. Our buddy Harvey calls it "hanging crepe": that mysterious funereal darkness that Christians spread, the gloom and doom of life, the concerned "sharing," the furrowed brows, the long faces. After all, sin and saving souls are serious business.

One friend, in charge of children's ministry at her very somber church, remembers bringing the puppet show up to the "Big People's Church" one Sunday. The one-liners were enormously funny, but they fell in the church like lead inside a tomb. The head pastor sat, arms crossed, a dark look on his face, totally unresponsive. The congregation followed the lead. But the new associate didn't know the rules, didn't know it wasn't OK to laugh in church and hooted throughout the entire performance.

As his howling, solo laugh echoed inside the cavernous sanctuary, my friend and her husband looked at each other, the realization dawning gradually: we have forgotten what it means to laugh. "The entire time we attended that church, we never once heard laughter except for that Sunday," she said. "Our motto was the hymn 'We'll Work 'Til Jesus Comes.'"

I believe God loves our laughter. I can't wait to get to heaven and hear his laugh. Perhaps his laughter is the real cause of wind, that inexplicable mystery puzzling students—and their mothers, when asked, "Where does wind come from?" Surely he laughs when baby piglets are born, when whales exhale as fast as a plane on takeoff, when giraffes stick out their tongues, when frogs catch flies. Surely he laughs when kittens play and children learn to talk. Surely he chuckles when daddies take off the baby's diaper and get sprayed. Surely he laughs . . .

Surely we can laugh too, then. Last week, Rich whisked me off to Chicago for our anniversary. One of his surprises was seeing *Blue Man Group,* an absolutely madcap display of rhythm and insanity and pure looniness on the part of three men, dressed in blue head masks and blue gloves and silly somber-looking shirts that actually . . . well, never mind, it would spoil the fun.

Though the Blue Men did not speak one word in the entire performance, I laughed until I cried. I put my head on my husband's shoulder and shook with laughter, wiping tears away. And I noticed that when I laugh, I feel God's presence. And I am more loving to others.

> ## TRAVELOGUE
>
> • *What sort of image did you grow up with about "Christians"? Could they have fun, or was that forbidden?*
>
> *How do any preconceived notions hinder you now?*

SERIOUS BUSINESS

Near the end of the long flight, the attendant announced that we would watch a comedy show. I was working, working, working—didn't want to waste a minute of time, my overdeveloped work ethic muscling aside play. Others' laughter caught my attention. First quiet chuckles, then out loud guffaws. I stuck the headset over my ears wondering if even I, great sober-sides, would find the show funny. Soon my sides ached and my eyes leaked from laughing.

A sociologist would have had a ball observing the flight. At their first trickles of escaping laughter, people glanced out of the corner of their eyes, checking: "Is anyone else laughing? Am I the only weirdo who thinks this is funny?" Finding similar reactions, the passengers relaxed in their seats, even daring to trade glances and swap smiles.

When we filed out of the plane, eye contact and an occasional grin testified to the success of humor in creating intimacy. Which makes its own point: things are much better shared with companions. A sidesplitting laugh-fest lasts much longer when others join in the fun.

But a permission process must occur within ourself to take time in the wilderness for fun. Today our high schoolers finished their finals and have nothing due or to do for four entire days except to show up at their part-time jobs for a few hours. They were ecstatic, planning adventures. My husband and I looked at one another, asking, "What must that feel like? If we don't work, we're in trouble. Imagine four days with no expectations." Planning in playtime makes no sense for the self-employed living on a shoestring. Unless they want to stay alive.

Unless, when we honor God's idea of rest, of Sabbath, of enjoyment, he steps up to the plate and keeps the work-ball in the air. Play, for many, becomes an issue of trust and comes more easily when releasing our pain into the hands of the One who intended to carry us and our pain all along. Fun in the wilderness is, after all, a matter of perspective: God is greater than all our turmoil, God is the only One who knows and holds our future, and we can lighten our grip after all. And enjoy the moment at hand.

A TOOL FOR PAIN

Greenville, South Carolina, embedded thought-provoking quotes into the sidewalk on its main street. Because of her unique niche in our world, they included one of Erma Bombeck's: "I've been on a constant diet for the last two decades. I've lost a total of 789 pounds. By all accounts I should be hanging from a charm bracelet."

Erma came along as one of the first, and best, humor writers, and America watched closely as she handled the news of her breast cancer, then kidney failure and transplant. Her trademark humor allowed her to interpret illness—her own and others'—for the world at large, and it carried her through to the very end of her life, effectively helping both her and her readers move through the valley of the shadow of death.

LIFE IS BEAUTIFUL

Perhaps the signature film displaying fun as a tool for traversing through tough times is *Life Is Beautiful*. When the father in the movie, Guido, played by Roberto Benigni, realizes that he, his wife and son will be interned in a concentration camp, with minimal chance of survival, he cooks up a game for his preschooler. Treating the entire internment experience as a contest arranged as a special treat for his son, Joshua, whose birthday party had been interrupted by the Gestapo, Guido explains the rules: Joshua must be quiet all day, not ask for his mommy and stay in hiding. All children are competing, and the first child to get a thousand points wins the grand prize: a ride in a real, life-size tank (Joshua's favorite toy). This movie elicits both grief and joy, horror and laughter, as well as encouragement and perspective for anyone needing a new outlook on life—or perhaps a little re-parenting.

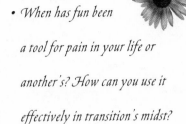

TRAVELOGUE

- *When has fun been a tool for pain in your life or another's? How can you use it effectively in transition's midst?*

- *Around whom do you laugh easily? Can you make time to laugh together during your wilderness?*

- *In what situations can you remember choosing to lighten your grip and relax into God?*

Fun is an excellent weapon over the enemy, seen in our lives as discouragement, depression, fear, anger and bitterness.

RELAXING IN THE WILDERNESS

When Jesus returned from his wilderness sojourn, he came back to a wedding, the ultimate ceremony that mocks the discouragement and darkness of transition. Maybe you don't have a wedding to celebrate, but there are many varieties of fun in the desert sun: something silly, like building a fort with your kids or just for yourself! Or a bubble bath, or your favorite carryout food, or a childhood delight, like jigsaw puzzles or board games, or playing kick the can, or chasing lightning bugs, or renting a paddle boat at a nearby lake, or going to the amusement park or skating rink (that should bring a laugh), or a bag of cotton candy and a walk, or . . . simple, clean, plain old fun can transform the journey. And our heart.

If we notice. If we let the mysterious process do its work.

It's puzzling, but when I speak, people seem to laugh. "Your home must be so much fun," an audience member once said. My heart quelled because my home wasn't exactly a barrel of monkeys. Once, a coordinator met one of my children and said, "Did you know that women laugh when your mom speaks?" My child did not know that—I just wasn't funny at home. Humor depends on perspective, and my task-oriented approach to life and family dried up any mirth faster than dew evaporates in the desert heat. My heart was as dry as beef jerky—and thousands of times heavier. Elizabeth Potier wrote in *Elle*, "It isn't life that weighs us down—it's the way we carry it."

My lack of laughter seemed in proportion to my lack of faith. But the wilderness is teaching me—that God is truly the Lord of the wasteland. He has shown himself quite capable of caring for me in the midst of sandstorm and melting sun. Increasingly, as I trust him more, my joy ratio rises. Though we are not through the desert yet, laughter comes more easily, fun more spontaneously.

And what a great option: choosing to find fun is one of God's wackiest tools and a wonderful juxtaposition to the wilderness—truly a grace point. If we must live in the desert, let's grab a shovel and build sand castles.

Wilderness Response

ACCOMPANIMENT PSALM

When the LORD brought back the captives to Zion,
  we were like men who dreamed.
Our mouths were filled with laughter,
  our tongues with songs of joy.
Then it was said among the nations,
  "The LORD has done great things for them."
The LORD has done great things for us,
  and we are filled with joy.

Restore our fortunes, O LORD,
  like streams in the Negev.
Those who sow in tears
  will reap with songs of joy.
He who goes out weeping,
  carrying seed to sow,
will return with songs of joy,
  carrying sheaves with him.

PSALM 126:1-6

DESERT READING

Remember the Sabbath day by keeping it holy. Six days you shall
labor and do all your work, but the seventh day is a Sabbath to
the LORD your God. On it you shall not do any work, neither you,
nor your son or daughter, nor your manservant or maidservant,
nor your animals, nor the alien within your gates. For in six days
the LORD made the heavens and the earth, the sea, and all that is
in them, but he rested on the seventh day. Therefore the LORD

blessed the Sabbath day and made it holy.
EXODUS 20:8-11

GUIDING SONG

O Happy Day

O happy day, that fixed my choice
On Thee, my Savior and my God!
Well may this glowing heart rejoice,
And tell its raptures all abroad.

O happy bond, that seals my vows
To him who merits all my love!
Let cheerful anthems fill his house,
While to that sacred shrine I move.

Now rest, my long divided heart,
Fixed on this blissful center, rest.
Here have I found a nobler part;
Here heavenly pleasures fill my breast.
WORDS: PHILIP DODDRIDGE, 1755
MUSIC: ANONYMOUS

REMEMBER YOUR JOURNEY

- Where do you want to see God create a grace point through fun in the desert? How can you assist by finding fun? What would that look like?

Still Point

Whatever they think I may have in the way of comfort and healing,

and I, who in the old days would have shrunk with fear

from any such charged encounter,

try to find something wise and hopeful to say to them,

only little by little coming to understand

that the most precious thing I have to give them

is not whatever words I find to say—

but simply whatever, spoken or unspoken,

I have in me of Christ,

which is also the most precious thing they have to give me.

All too rarely, I regret to say, my search has taken me also

to a sacred and profoundly silent place inside myself,

where it is less that I pray than that,

to paraphrase Saint Paul,

the Holy Spirit, I believe, prays within me and for me

with sighs too deep for words (Romans 8:26).

FREDERICK BUECHNER

II
....

Choosing to Not Forget

And He has said to me,

"My grace is sufficient for you, for power is perfected in weakness."

Most gladly, therefore, I will rather boast about my weakness,

that the power of Christ may dwell in me.

2 Corinthians 12:9 NASB

This week, meeting with a friend, I spilled some family-related fear. My friend pointed me to God's faithfulness with goodness and humor. Later, eating our cookies, I showed her my fortune: "Family relationships will improve with time." I expected her to discount the words—ha, ha, a fortune cookie.

Instead, she cheered. "Yes! That's right. That's the Lord speaking. His voice comes from some amazing places. He's giving you something to hold on to, Jane. He will heal that family member."

WHAT MEAN THESE STONES?

After forty years of wilderness wandering, the Israelites were at last ready to cross the Jordan and move into the Promised Land. Through Joshua, God said, "As soon as the priests who carry the ark of the LORD—the LORD of all the earth—set foot in the Jordan, its waters flowing downstream will be cut off and stand up in a heap" (Joshua 3:13). God also commanded twelve people from the twelve tribes of Israel to take up a stone from the middle of the river, right out from under the priests' feet, and haul the rocks to the other side. The place where they slept that night would be the stones' permanent home, a memorial "to serve as a sign among you" (Joshua 4:1-6). When their children asked, "What do these stones mean?" the adults were to recount the story of God's power and deliverance.

They were to tell them, "Israel crossed the Jordan on dry ground. For the LORD your God dried up the Jordan before you until you had crossed over. The LORD your God did to the Jordan just what he had done to the Red Sea when he dried it up before us until we had crossed over. He did this so that all the peoples of the earth might know that the hand of the LORD is powerful and so that you might always fear the LORD your God" (Joshua 4:22-24).

Like the Israelites, we build altars of remembrance composed of lots of stones. "That silly slip of paper is a stone to build the altar," said my friend that fortune-cookie day. "We need materials to work with when it comes to our faith."

A CASE FOR STONES

Yesterday, I dragged out my old briefcase. Layers of dust cloaked my well-worn companion, filling in the dents and nicks. I had replaced it hastily, never totally emptying it. Judging by the contents, our last travels together had been in 1999 and 2000.

Remembering. Those were our first freelance years. Apprehension gnawed every available thought into bits, fragmenting my attention span, preoccupying my heart. A smile, then tears, came as I sorted through the unexpected keepsake "stones" inside.

A tollway receipt from that first fall. Totaling the month's speaking in advance, I saw we'd be short financially. A group coordinator promptly called, needing a speaker for two meetings—would I consider it?

An encouraging note from a woman I'd met through a Write-to-Publish writers' conference, who later set me up as her church's retreat speaker. And that misplaced Steak-n-Shake gift certificate—a prize at a women's event in Chattanooga. I'd gone there after their coordinator heard a long-postponed radio interview, then invited me to facilitate the weekend. My mother and a best friend attended with me, and we'd had a glorious time. Best of all, God had moved women's hearts at the retreat.

A matchbook from a hotel five hours away. The church had called, we scheduled the day, but "We can't pay much, Jane," they'd warned. Still, they'd secured donors to purchase a book from me for every woman attending; they'd hidden the books under each seat, then like Oprah announced the gift. Moreover, some of those women longed to write and began acting on their dreams. That day of ministry continues to bear fruit.

Notepads from a resort tell another story of God's faithfulness. I wrote to a pastor's wife I'd met the prior year, wondering if she needed a speaker. The day before receiving it, not expecting my letter, she said to her committee, "A pastor's wife I met does retreats and writes books. I wonder how to contact her."

My briefcase was God's scrapbook, detailing his wilderness resourcing. My altar grows ever higher as the stones heap up. I bow my head, eyes damp, and remember God's steadfast care. It is enough to take to the bank.

Our futures are not in our keeping or our most clever scheming; they are in God's hands, and remembering our stories helps us find him again in the darkness of the desert's uncertainty, doubt and fear. Our memory stones build the altar of faith, where we worship God.

REMEMBERING AND RESCUING

We hunger for story because story connects with our heart, giving us a lens through which to examine the way we live. The problem? It is much easier to focus on another's story, a sitcom or a saga involving famous people than to move from the public to the private. We are more comfortable dissecting the high profile because it saves face—we do not have to be

TRAVELOGUE

•Where have you seen

reminders of God's faithfulness,

His lovingkindness? Whether

your journey has involved

financial, relational, emotional

or physical difficulty, how has

God sown stones of remembrance?

• What story have you hidden

from others, from yourself? Can

you write it now, in the safety of

your journal? Why do you think

you have kept silent?

• What is God telling you about

your story? About his heart

for you?

vulnerable ourselves. As long as it pertains to media royalty or even our neighbor, the most trivial information—or even gossip—interests us.

Our need for story becomes our downfall until we shift the camera to our own soul, because the value in story is that it reconnects our fast-paced living with our woundedness, with our heart, with our longings and needs.

In the desert, after finding the survivor, search and rescue teams debrief to learn from the survivor's mistakes and skills. Was the map wrong? The guide incorrect? Were trail markers missing? Where did you go off course? How did you stay alive? What resources, food, water did you find, and where?

Telling our story can save lives, time, anguish. This is why storytelling is so vital at recovery groups—so others can listen, learn and live. Our stories give people a chance to grieve their stories and their loss of innocence, life and love. Stories reassure us that we are not alone and crack the bondage of silence, the covenant of burial to which we have agreed all these years, the contract of secrecy with the enemy. Jan Meyers writes:

Our stories are given to us by God; they are never meant to impact only us. . . . As we live our lives in the Valley of Achor (the "Valley of Trouble," Hosea 2:15), consumed with our own stories and the losses they hold, we lose sight of the majestic way God weaves our paths with others in the desert. We make the Valley of Achor an endless door of revisited sorrow rather than allowing God to transform it into a door of hope as we bump up against other people.

One woman had never talked about her adolescent addiction and promiscuity. She bottomed out after awakening next to a young man she despised when sober. During our retreat, she gathered the courage to share her past with close friends, and later that week someone asked if she would give her testimony to a group of students. With great fear, she spoke. Young women wept, found grace and hope, and God gained glory—because he is a God of forgiveness and restoration!—through her telling the story of her lostness and of God finding her.

Another woman confessed to her small group about a long-ago abortion. For a quarter-century she told no one except the father, and he after the fact. She'd lugged her shame and pain like a backpack full of bricks, acting out the agony through multiple marriages, quick pregnancies and childbearing, and speedy divorces. Sharing her story brought her healing and forgiveness and freed others to explore their own memories. Stories—testimonies—do not glorify our pain and missteps but testify to God's deliverance.

REMEMBER WHEN?

Perhaps you have not dared to remember incidents from your past because of the pain and shame that arise. It's important to recognize that the women mentioned in this chapter first shared their stories in places of sanctuary where they were loved, where their pain and tears were honored, and where they would receive grace, not judgment. Indiscriminate disclosure may reap more harm on a broken heart or spirit.

For me, remembering often starts in time alone with God or in the security of my journal. Remembering continues then in the presence of a trusted advisor, pastor, friend or a small group, where depth and respect have been established, as well as some general guidelines for receiving another's story. Parameters might include

- not trying to correct the person's mistake,

- not offering advice,

- listening for pain or shame

- asking clarifying questions, such as, "Say some more about what that felt like, or about your anger there, or . . . " and

- remembering that grace, understanding, forgiveness and prayer are the best responses to one another's stories.

Inappropriate reactions, requiring us to look within for their reasons, include remaining silent, changing the subject, moving to a safer or more comfortable place conversationally, directing horror toward the person rather than expressing sorrow over the pain. We could ask, alone or in a group, "What made me uncomfortable? Why did I need to distance, change the subject, stay silent? Why do I come across as judgmental?"

Once, when I relayed some background to two dear and trustworthy but relatively new friends, they simply wept. They looked at me through tears and said, "I'm so sorry, Jane. I'm so sorry. It is not supposed to be that way. God longed for so much more for you." And that was perfect. I didn't need advice on how to fix a long-term fracture, not then. I just needed for my story to be honored.

REMEMBER WHAT?

"Remember." "Do not forget." These commands fill the Scriptures, with the word *remember,* or some form thereof, appearing 264 times in the King James Version. They rang in the Israelites' ears and sang out in their psalms and songs. The storytelling tradition of the Jews reaches back to God's admonitions to tell their story, his story—his calling from Eden and the saga of their bondage, escape and desert travels.

"Remember your journey," says Micah, "that you may know the righteous acts of the LORD" (Micah 6:5).

Stories of God's deliverance and provisions strengthened the Israelites. In times of slavery, exile, war and peace, they remembered. Their deliverance from the Egyptians became the benchmark memory, the point of comparison. As if God says, "Did I not do this? Well, then, if I could deliver you from bondage with such power and might, I can surely do _____ for you." We could almost fill in the blank with our need.

And so do we also remember God's faithfulness and provision in order to move on, not to re-suffer but to look at the redemption, the release, the reclamation! We remember our pain not to dwell on it but to celebrate God's healing.

> I remember my affliction and my wandering,
>> the bitterness and gall.
> I well remember them,
>> and my soul is downcast within me.
> Yet this I call to mind
>> and therefore I have hope:
>
> Because of the LORD's great love we are not consumed,
>> for his compassions never fail.
> They are new every morning;
>> great is your faithfulness.
> I say to myself, "The LORD is my portion;
>> therefore I will wait for him."
>
> The LORD is good to those whose hope is in him,
>> to the one who seeks him;
> it is good to wait quietly
>> for the salvation of the LORD. (Lamentations 3:19-26)

REMEMBERING RESTORES FAITH

One Sunday at church, our worship leader framed the service around people's faith journeys. From gray-haired seniors to children, testimony flowed of God's love in rock-hard places, his provisions in financial peril, his grace in awkward spaces. I left afterward, believing once again that God could do anything, because these people had the courage to remember aloud their travels. The stories of the saints bring renewal, build faith, give courage to walk on, to trust, to obey.

Remembering brings comfort. Called "the Great Hallel," meaning "praise," in Jewish liturgy, Psalm 136 is an antiphonal psalm, a call and response, every verse beginning with a piece of history for the Israelites—a memory!—and ending with "his love endures forever."

What do we learn from another's story or from a story in Scripture or in a movie? The creation story in Genesis 1, for instance, tells us that darkness is not emptiness but that life can rise out of that void; the Spirit of God specializes in moving over the face of the darkness (the waters).

TRAVELOGUE

• *Journal about a place of provision where God provided for you beyond what you asked or imagined (Ephesians 3:20).*

• *Where have you seen God begin to heal? Can you revisit difficult circumstances in order to celebrate freedom? Can you pull up on your heart's screen the "affliction and wandering" (Lamentations 3:19-26), remembering God's deliverance?*

• *When has remembering restored faith or brought comfort, whether another's story or your own?*

And life will come out of this time that seems dark as death.

Our local chapter of Christian Youth Theater performed *The Little Princess,* which has some emotionally wrenching scenes. Later, we remembered people weeping, from director to crew to cast to audience. Why? Because it is a story of love, and loss, and finding love again—and so many people have loved and lost, loved and never found again, or never loved at all and lived out of their wounds.

FORGETTING

But we are so quick to forget. I remember ongoing friction with a former boyfriend—we both felt betrayed, though I can't remember why now. At some point, we decided that we could be civil to one another, if not friends then polite acquaintances. However, when we saw each other at a college function, the cold masks slid instantly over our faces. It wasn't until later that I remembered, "Oh yeah, we weren't mad at each other anymore."

In a larger way, we are so prone to forget God's work on our behalf. The Scriptures say of Israel, "They forgot the God who saved them, who had done great things" (Psalm 106:21). "After that whole generation had been gathered to their fathers, another generation grew up, who knew neither the LORD nor what he had done for Israel" (Judges 2:10). Why didn't they know? Did they abandon their stories so quickly? Because they didn't remember, didn't hand down the stories, the people left God, abandoned the faith and worshiped the false gods of the people around them.

We choose to remember, because if we don't remember and share our stories, our faith is extinct, not surviving after us. "The journey that isn't shared dies young," said Anne Sexton.

And we ask God to remember. "Remember, Lord," begs the psalmist in Psalm 89, "how fleeting my life. . . . O LORD where is your former great love, which in your faithfulness you swore to David? Remember, LORD, how your servant has been mocked" (vv. 47, 49-50). And somehow, in reminding God, our remembering brings rest and trust: "Praise be to the LORD forever! Amen and amen" (v. 52).

"Jesus, remember me when you come into your kingdom," pleaded the thief on the cross next to Christ (Luke 23:42). And we plead, as well. "Jesus, remember me."

REMEMBER WHO YOU ARE

Desert delirium can wipe our memory slate clean: we forget not only God's presence at our side but also our own identity. Something about the wilderness forces the question: who have I been, who am I now in the face of this difficulty, this tragedy, this present and future unknown?

In *The Lion King,* Simba is a young lion set to be the next king. When his father is murdered, Simba, blaming himself, flees. While in exile, he moves through an elaborate, don't-worry-be-happy ritual in order to forget his disappointments, his failure, his identity and his calling. His father appears to him in a dream, growling in a regal voice, "Remember who you are." The voice echoes in the wake of his desert doubts. Simba awakens from his "hakuna matata" living and embraces his heritage and calling.

"Remember who you are." Who are you, without the lies of the past, without the untruths and half-truths you believed about yourself as a child and teenager, without the brokenness of living in a fallen world? Who are we, who did God create us to be, what does he see in us? Is what you know most deeply about yourself that you are loved and accepted by God, that God delights in you?

In the book *The Bourne Identity*, a young man is found floating in a storm at sea with two bullet holes in him, and he comes to consciousness minus his memory. He remembers instinctively his abilities and uncanny strength but not his name or profession. He remembers facts—"At this altitude I could run flat-out for a mile before my hands start shaking. Now why would I know that and not know who I am?" He learns he is a man of multiple identities and passports, but not why. As he accesses more of his past, a past full of violence and espionage, he also encounters his lost heart. He discovers good parts of himself—his integrity, compassion, loyalty, protectiveness.

But it requires a wilderness to reclaim the parts of him lost in the high-caliber training of his past. By remembering the good and the hurtful parts of his story, he can choose to relinquish those damaging sides, honing and holding on to his good heart.

Sometimes it takes a wilderness to remember who God has called us to be. A desert sifts out the falsehoods of our past (you are not lovely, you will not amount to anything, you don't deserve any attention) and lets the God of the desert restore us fully to his image, his dream of us.

Choosing to not forget becomes a grace point in the wilderness, because God will never forget us. "Can a mother forget the baby at her breast and have no compassion on the child she has borne? Though she may forget, I will not forget you! See, I have engraved you on the palms of my hands" (Isaiah 49:15-16).

And so we remember and find grace, and God anew, in the desert.

Wilderness Response

ACCOMPANIMENT PSALM

Praise the LORD, O my soul;
    all my inmost being, praise his holy name.
Praise the LORD, O my soul,
    and forget not all his benefits—
who forgives all your sins
    and heals all your diseases,
who redeems your life from the pit
    and crowns you with love and compassion,
who satisfies your desires with good things,
    so that your youth is renewed like the eagle's.

The LORD works righteousness
    and justice for all the oppressed.

He made known his ways to Moses,
    his deeds to the people of Israel. . . .
As a father has compassion on his children,
    so the LORD has compassion on those who fear him;
for he knows how we are formed,
    he remembers that we are dust.

PSALM 103:1-7, 13-14

DESERT READING

Moses said to the people, "Remember this day in which you went
out from Egypt, from the house of slavery; for by a powerful hand
the LORD brought you out from this place. . . . It shall be when the
LORD brings you to the land . . . which He swore to your fathers

to give you, a land flowing with milk and honey, that you shall observe this rite in this month. . . . For seven days you shall eat unleavened bread, and on the seventh day there shall be a feast to the LORD. . . . You shall tell your son on that day, saying, 'It is because of what the LORD did for me when I came out of Egypt.' And it shall serve as a sign to you on your hand, and as a reminder on your forehead, that the law of the LORD may be in your mouth; for with a powerful hand the LORD brought you out of Egypt."

EXODUS 13:3-9 NASB

GUIDING SONG

O God, Our Help in Ages Past

O God, our help in ages past, our hope for years to come,
Our shelter from the stormy blast, and our eternal home!

Before the hills in order stood, or earth received her frame,
From everlasting, thou art God, to endless years the same.

A thousand ages, in thy sight, are like an evening gone;
Short as the watch that ends the night, before the rising sun.

WORDS: ISAAC WATTS, 1719
MUSIC: ATTRIBUTED TO WILLIAM CROFT, 1709

REMEMBER YOUR JOURNEY

- As you remember your story, invite Jesus into the scenes. Watch his eyes fill with love, and see him receive your pain. Let him give you healing in that place.

Still Point

O come, O come, Emmanuel,

and ransom captive Israel,

That mourns in lonely exile here

until the Son of God appears.

"O COME, O COME, EMMANUEL"

12

....

CHOOSING FREEDOM

Grace and peace be yours in abundance.

1 PETER 1:2

Set in 1940s Louisiana, the movie *A Lesson Before Dying* opens with a young man, Jefferson (Mehki Phifer), jauntily walking to the river to fish. Background music hints of upcoming change in his carefree life. Two friends pick him up in their car and convince him to stop at a liquor store with them. While Jefferson waits in the doorway, the buddies try to wheedle the owner into putting their wine on credit. The owner refuses. Gunfire flashes. The friends and the storeowner are dead. Jefferson, found on the scene, is framed in court, though innocent of murder. (When a white man dies, a black man goes to jail, the movie explains.) His defense lawyer states in his closing argument:

> Gentlemen of the jury, I ask you to look at my client. Is that a *man* you see sittin' there? Would you call this a man? A fool perhaps—a fool who is not aware of right and wrong. A fool who stood by and watched this happen, not having the sense to run. No, gentlemen, not a man. What you see sitting there is a *thing* that acts on command, a thing to hold the handle of a plow, to chop your wood

and pull your corn. But not a thing capable of planning a robbery or a murder. Gentlemen of the jury, who would be hurt if you took this life? If you convicted this boy, who would be hurt?

He points to the boy's adoptive grandmother, who sits in the courtroom with a broken heart, then closes his plea:

For God's sake be merciful. He is innocent of all charges brought against him. But let us for a moment say he was not. Even so, what justice would there be to take his life? Justice, gentlemen? You might just as soon put a hog in the electric chair as this. Just a poor dumb hog.

At the sentence to Jefferson's self-worth, his face falls, his head and body slump; the prison doors slam shut on his soul. His grandmother, horrified that her child believes the worst about himself—a death edict of the heart—enlists the help of the local teacher to begin meeting with Jefferson. To what end? That he might "die with some dignity," going to the chair not as a hog to slaughter but as a man. More than lessons in esteem and positive thinking, their sessions become a tutorial for the spirit, chronicling both men's choice to journey to freedom. Though Jefferson's trip leads to the electric chair, he walks there as a whole man, a free man.

LET MY PEOPLE GO

Since Joseph's death, the Israelites waited hundreds of years in Egypt for God's promise to be fulfilled. "I am about to die," said Joseph. "But God will surely come to your aid and take you out of this land to the land he promised on oath to Abraham, Isaac and Jacob" (Genesis 50:24).

They waited and multiplied, in spite of oppression and open dislike from the Egyptians who reasoned, "They're too numerous for us! We must oppress them or they will get bigger, join our enemies, fight us and leave" (Exodus 1:9-10 paraphrased). Freedom was the last thing they wanted for the Israelites; Egypt built a powerful nation on the backs of their slaves.

But the Hebrews lived in the shadow of God's protection, experiencing the liberty of growth in spite of hardship. Growth in difficult situations always threatens the enemy.

For God, freedom is the bottom line.

> The LORD said [to Moses], "I have indeed seen the misery of my people in Egypt. I have heard them crying out because of their slave drivers, and I am concerned about their suffering. So I have come down to rescue them. . . . And now the cry of the Israelites has reached me, and I have seen the way the Egyptians are oppressing them. So now, go. I am sending you to Pharaoh to bring my people the Israelites out of Egypt." (Exodus 3:7-10)

This has been God's message from the very beginning—freedom. From the Garden of Eden to the empty tomb, from Egyptian oppression to sin's captivity and darkness, God's cry of deliverance is unchanging: "Let my people go." Whether from bondage to the past or to pain or to the present, whether to false idols or to ill-chosen relationships, whether to another's labeling (as in Jefferson's case) or to our own choices, God has provided liberation.

Freedom is an internal state of heart and mind, independent of life circumstances, past or present; and while the future itself cannot chain us, anxiety about the future enslaves. Circumstances may imprison our body, but no one can incarcerate our soul unless we give them power over us.

Jamey's medical history reads like Murphy's Law, but when I last saw her, she said, "My body is a challenge, but my heart is free." She refuses to be caged emotionally or spiritually in the confines of myriad physical problems.

Claudia's life and feelings revolved around an alcoholic for years. Though she came to Christ somewhere in her journey, she still lived each

TRAVELOGUE

• *When or how have you found freedom despite external circumstances?*

• *Who or what are your slave drivers (Exodus 3:7)? Think of heart, mind, body, work, church, duties, spirituality.*

• *When do you cry out? How does it appear? Where have you sought freedom, only to find another trap?*

• *Consider the "Truth Talk" passages. How do these counter what you have believed, or lived, all these years?*

moment preoccupied with her husband, his drinking and its ramifications on their family. Finally, on the verge of a breakdown, she began attending a support group and learned to detach from his craziness and get well herself. Choosing to stay married, her husband's active alcoholism no longer traps Claudia; she has found freedom to live in its midst.

FALSE FREEDOM

In our elusive quest for freedom, it is easy to misdirect our search. Denise, unhappy in her marriage and feeling trapped as a mother, engrossed herself in antiquing. She met an attractive divorcé. At first, the affair felt like liberty, an escape from Denise's misery, but it was a foil for real freedom. Instead of increasing her liberation, the affair increased her bondage and compromised everything she and her husband believed, wounding many.

Cathy left home at eighteen, vowing to be free of the pain in her family of origin. Unfortunately, her search for freedom got snagged on the spindle of anger, and rather than living unfettered, pain pinioned her for years. Her life deteriorated, emphasizing the tremendous cost of trying to escape the pain. Her freedom journey began when she sought help for her childhood anguish and the subsequent demolition of relationships that grew out of her anger and abandonment issues.

We jettison the freedom God offers in other ways too. Consuming pastimes, obsessive relationships, neurotic exercise, compulsive caregiving, mega-control, addictive living, conflict avoidance, even religious service—all are means of seeking love and freedom that can waylay and snare us in the very process. We also give up our freedom to choose our heart by bowing out, letting others decide for us who and how we will be.

For years, I could not express anger or hurt positively. I practiced "bury and blow," giving up control to those very feelings. Though I knew the Lord and tried to serve him, I was imprisoned, with no clue how to break that bondage or what Christ meant when he said, "You will know the truth, and the truth will set you free" (John 8:32).

TRUTH TALK: THE TRUTH SHALL SET YOU FREE

What is the truth?

- *God's love for us never ends; it stretches from the beginning of time through all eternity:* "I have loved you with an everlasting love" (Jeremiah 31:3).

- *He's never going to let us go:* "Never will I leave you; never will I forsake you" (Hebrews 13:5).

- *God flings our sins at opposite ends of the earth when he forgives us:* "As far as the east is from the west, so far has he removed our transgressions from us" (Psalm 103:12).

- *Absolutely nothing will wedge us away from God:* Nothing can "separate us from the love of God that is in Christ Jesus our Lord" (Romans 8:32-39).

FEAR OF FREEDOM

How were the Israelites imprisoned? Bondage and abuse break and bind our spirit. Even after deliverance from the Egyptian taskmasters, they had to be freed from their past, their cringing fear. They had to learn to live as chosen people, loved enough to be ransomed in such a movie-script way.

But the rescue alone didn't set them free. The wasteland became a spiritual boot camp for the rescued nation as they learned to live free. Free of abuse, of servitude, of shackles and impossible demands. But beyond that, their deliverance again had to do with trust. At the skirt of the Promised Land, they were so full of fear that they would not enter. They believed the wrong voices; fear set them back forty years, costing the lives of an entire generation.

For us, as well, a primary hindrance to freedom is fear—just as some people are so afraid of falling and breaking a hip that they tense up when they move and eventually just stop moving. Muscles atrophy from fear, which makes falling all the more likely when they do move.

We are no different spiritually. We are afraid of being misunderstood, of having our feelings hurt, our heart broken or our self-esteem damaged by failing, so like walking on ice in stilettos, we shut down, tense up, contract our heart and live bound. We're afraid of other people, of the unknown, of being found out ("If people knew the truth about me . . . "). Perhaps our greatest fear is of being inadequate, insufficient—that, and not being loved. Our soul-muscles wither in response to our fear.

Yet the Scriptures remind us, "He heals the brokenhearted and binds up their wounds" (Psalm 147:3).

What does this tell us? That heartbreak is inevitable. And so is the binding up of those hearts—if we are looking in the right place for the healing.

This fear is a type of death for us, until we direct ourself to Christ, who "suffered death, so that by the grace of God he might taste death for everyone" (Hebrews 2:9). And then what? He frees "those who all their lives were held in slavery by their fear of death" (Hebrews 2:15).

PARADOX OF FREEDOM

"It is for freedom that Christ has set us free. Stand firm, then, and do not let yourselves be burdened again by a yoke of slavery" (Galatians 5:1), but take on the yoke of Christ (Matthew 11:28-30). Here again is the paradox of faith: Christ breaks the yoke of slavery, then asks us to put our necks in the same yoke with his—and he will pull all the weight.

Even so, we have to resist the strains against our freedom. How do we stand firm, fighting against other entrapments, without becoming self-centered and self-protective?

Remembering God's Word helps when we're tempted to be

enslaved by anger, self-pity, another's expectations, superhuman standards, or just by others' approval or disapproval. What has God said about freedom for us? Isaiah 58:6 says, "Is this not the fast which I choose, to loosen the bonds of wickedness, to undo the bands of the yoke, and to let the oppressed go free, and break every yoke?" (NASB). Jesus reminds us that he is our freedom: "If therefore the Son shall make you free, you shall be free indeed" (John 8:36; see also Exodus 21:2; 1 Corinthians 7:21-23; Galatians 3:26-29).

Christianity is a great oxymoron—complete opposites reside next to one another with perplexing, confounding regularity. The weak are strong, the poor are rich, the humble are exalted. The lion lies beside the lamb. And captives are set free by giving themselves away to God. We who have spent our years protecting ourselves, keeping ourselves safe, living low-risk lives—we are called to give, now, give ourselves completely away, to live as "God's slaves" (1 Peter 2:16 NET). We've given God our heart, our life is his; if he is good and trustworthy, then we have nothing to fear. And freedom's breath comes that much easier.

But wait—isn't this giving away of ourself precisely what we're fighting? Meet again the resurgence of panic. Fear howls and assails, and we wonder, *What am I doing?* Gaining freedom by giving ourselves to *anyone* makes no sense whatsoever, we tell ourselves.

Right. No sense at all. Unless the recipient, the One to whom we give ourselves, is Christ, the very One who gave himself (and all of heaven) up for us. For our freedom.

When we stop living for ourself, stop living to protect ourself, our bondage breaks. Our protector is God himself, the mighty warrior who rejoices over us, who guards every breath we breathe and counts the hairs on our head. When he is fighting for us, then we are free. But what do we do with that news?

FREEDOM AVOIDANCE

Sometimes we avoid that freedom, like Brooks in Stephen King's *Rita Hayworth and the Shawshank Redemption.* He'd lived so long and amenably on the inside of the prison that, when released, he couldn't live without bars. Within weeks, he'd hung himself at his halfway house, the very place meant to prepare him for life on the outside. The prison protected Brooks—as our self-made prisons protect us. We chain ourselves to shame, resentment, anger, unforgiveness, labels, the abuse of the past, wealth, power, status. We believe lies that keep us incarcerated:

- Don't trust—don't trust *anyone.*
- Guard yourself; life isn't safe—make sure you don't get hurt.
- You are not good enough, lovely enough, interesting enough, so you must work hard, obey all rules, earn your keep and your salvation too.
- Do everything perfectly.
- Or, just forget trying. Do your own thing. It doesn't matter anyway because you can't make the grade.

Regardless of where we've come from, freedom is on God's agenda for our heart. Moses was eighty when he turned in obedience to follow God's call to freedom—it's never too late to be free!

What a deal—freedom because of obedience. "I will run in the path of your commands, for you have set my heart free" (Psalm 119:32). Freedom in the outback comes from choosing: love over withdrawal, repentance over resentment, peacemaking over anger, risk over safety, forgiveness over fighting.

THE MARK OF FREEDOM

Christ, like Moses, was born into a world of servitude—a world where foreign ruling powers held sway over people's hearts and lives. At his death the political situation had changed very little—but the heart had broken free. Christ, born as a servant, was the freest man who ever lived. Free because, in the midst of the worst trials the wilderness could dish out, he chose to trust, to obey. To love.

Our freedom is marked by our ability to love, not our ability to keep the rules (Galatians 5:13-14). It is marked by our ability to love and live wholly "in spite of the data," as my friend Suzie says. Despite the fact that we will be hurt, rejected, disappointed. Regardless of the fact of our own—and others'—disappointing human tendencies to fail. In spite of the truth: that the world is messed up, that our loving may fall short of the mark, and that others might very well hurt us in response. Loving, in spite of the data, is the mark of our freedom.

Luke 7:36-50 tells of a "sinful" woman who tracked Jesus down at the home of a Pharisee, a rule-keeper named Simon. The woman's sin is presumed to be prostitution, and her gumption was enormous at daring to seek Christ in the home of a law-abiding host. Simon opened his home to Christ but without standard hospitality, the signature of love—a kiss and a foot washing.

But this woman poured fragrant oil over Jesus, anointing him, kissing his feet and washing them with her tears. She of all people knew she could neither earn nor deserve Christ's love and forgiveness; society told her that, the law told her that, every time she dared to look into another's eyes they told her that. Though she knew people's opinions of her, she refused to be enslaved by them and was unafraid to crash the party at self-righteous Simon's.

Somehow, she discovered the extravagant grace of God. She embodied Jesus' words, which we find in Matthew 10:8, "Freely you have received, freely give." She who gave everything did so because she'd received everything, freely.

TRAVELOGUE

• *Why have you chosen*

to stay in the shackles when

freedom is offered?

• *Share a freedom dream or*

experience.

• *What has hindered your loving*

in the past? Of what, or whom,

are you afraid?

• *When have you found the*

freedom of loving others with

Christ's love?

But Simon . . . Simon was enslaved by his own righteousness. He'd never needed to receive much from another—certainly not forgiveness; as a Pharisee he prided himself on getting the law straight and adhering to its technicalities. In the process, he lost his heart. "He who is forgiven little loves little," Jesus told him (Luke 7:47). Self-righteous people rarely radiate much joy or love—they've never known the extravagance of forgiveness—and Simon was no exception.

The woman had lived a life of shame and wantonness, a life worthy of stoning according to Old Testament law, yet she was freed by Christ's love. Free from her past, her bondage, her heart-destitution, to love again. To love with Christ's love. To love Christ, with Christ's own love.

And there again is irony. Even as I consider that we are set free to love Christ with Christ's love, I ask myself, *Is this right? Can this be?* We love God not with our love but with the love he gives us! Talk about freedom—we don't even have to manipulate or manufacture our love. "God has poured out his love into our heart by the Holy Spirit" (Romans 5:5). He gives love to us so we can love him back. This is a no-lose deal for us, this side of heaven. It cost God, it cost Christ, but all we have to do to be free is . . . receive.

What astounding truth: when I am loving others with Christ's love, I don't have to fear rejection or even being hurt by another. I am not the one being rejected—it is Christ. Nor do I have to fear depletion of that love as long as I am resting and refilling in the wilderness. I am free to love passionately, to give joyfully, in spite of the possibility of pain in the offering, because it is Christ's love. And it is his love to which they will respond. Not mine. So when I love freely, live freely, then Christ is loving and living through me, and others see his beauty. God *longs* and intends to love others through the beauty of our loving.

The Freedom Fight

But the fight is far from over in this world. Good novels, and life itself, have both protagonist (the Deliverer) and antagonist (the Enemy). God paints a plain picture of warfare in Scripture. We have a very real, though often unrecognized, foe who would like to see the wilderness destroy us. This same adversary trained the cross hair on Christ while he was in the desert (Luke 3:21-22; 4:1-13). Christ teaches us to pray that we'd be delivered from the evil one (Matthew 6:13). Peter says, "Your enemy the devil prowls around like a roaring lion looking for someone to devour" (1 Peter 5:8). He prefaces his warning with the injunction, "Be self-controlled and alert." Keep awake, in other words. Smarten up. This is not innocuous talk—Christians in the early church knew the enemy preyed on them in the guise of religious opposition as well as Satan.

Freedom, this most precious gift granted by God through Christ's death and resurrection, is precisely the hot button for the enemy. He does not want us to live free. He prowls about, ravenous to destroy, to pull us to pieces. And in the wilderness, we are easy pickin's because the wilderness can be hazardous to our health and our faith.

I don't look for the devil behind every problem. But he is real. Just before a major holiday, at the start of a new recording project for our ministry, with one month left to finish this book and in the throes of a major mailing, our computers went crazy, every printer quit working, and despondency from other issues hit us so hard we weren't sure we could hold our life and family together. As I lay in bed that night praying, my heart awoke, finally, with the truth: this was enemy fire. If Satan could shred our family right then, he could destroy our work and calling and any good God might do through us. (And even as I typed this, my cursor disappeared and my computer screen froze.)

TRAVELOGUE

• *When have you experienced the victory of Christ fighting for your freedom against the Enemy?*

We must take up the sword of the Spirit, whether in the wilderness or just passing through life. Christ has broken Satan's hold over us and his power in this world. When we call on Christ's name and rely on his blood to cover and protect us, Satan is bound. Hebrews 2:14 states that "by his death [Christ destroyed] him who holds the power of death— that is, the devil." James writes: "Submit yourselves, then, to God. Resist the devil, and he will flee from you" (James 4:7).

One of the subdefinitions of *liberty* in my dictionary is "the power of choice." Freedom becomes our choice, our amazing grace point, in the wilderness.

Wilderness Response

ACCOMPANIMENT PSALM

He reached down from on high and took hold of me;
    he drew me out of deep waters.
He rescued me from my powerful enemy,
    from my foes, who were too strong for me.
They confronted me in the day of my disaster,
    but the LORD was my support.
He brought me out into a spacious place;
    he rescued me because he delighted in me.

PSALM 18:16-19

DESERT READING

The Spirit of the Sovereign LORD is on me,
    because the LORD has anointed me
    to preach good news to the poor.
He has sent me to bind up the brokenhearted,
    to proclaim freedom for the captives
    and release from darkness for the prisoners,
to proclaim the year of the LORD's favor
    and the day of vengeance of our God,
to comfort all who mourn,
    and provide for those who grieve in Zion—
to bestow on them a crown of beauty
    instead of ashes,
the oil of gladness
    instead of mourning,
and a garment of praise

instead of a spirit of despair.
They will be called oaks of righteousness,
  a planting of the LORD
   for the display of his splendor.
ISAIAH 61:1-3

GUIDING SONG

Come, Thou Long-Expected Jesus

Come, Thou Long-Expected Jesus,
Born to set thy people free;
From our fears and sins release us,
Let us find our rest in thee.

Israel's strength and consolation,
Hope of all the earth thou art;
Dear desire of every nation,
Joy of every longing heart.

Born thy people to deliver,
Born a child and yet a King,
Born to reign in us forever,
Now thy gracious kingdom bring.
WORDS: CHARLES WESLEY, 1744
MUSIC: ROWLAND H. PRICHARD, 1830

REMEMBER YOUR JOURNEY

• What will it look like to live free in this wilderness of transition? When and how will you choose freedom as a grace point?

Still Point

The ancient rabbis teach that on the seventh day,

God created mehuna—tranquility, serenity, peace, and repose—rest,

in the deepest possible sense of fertile, healing stillness.

Until the Sabbath, creation was unfinished.

Only after the birth of mehuna, only with tranquility and rest,

was the circle of creation made full and complete. . . .

Sabbath implies a willingness to be surprised by unexpected grace,

to partake of those potent moments when creation renews itself,

when what is finished inevitably recedes,

and the sacred forces of healing astonish us with

the unending promise of love and life.

WAYNE MULLER, *SABBATH*

13

....

WORSHIP IN
TRANSITION'S WILDERNESS

Let us then approach the throne of grace with confidence,
so that we may receive mercy and find grace to help us in our time of need.

HEBREWS 4:16

$\mathcal{D}$ragging out of bed, I pushed my hand to my sternum. My breath lurched at the familiar crushing feeling. I was finding it hard to breathe in the wilderness, as though living at high altitude, never certain how my family would make it through the day, let alone the month or year.

And it was Sunday, the day the heartbreak of this change punctured me most keenly. This new ministry threw our Sunday morning routines into catch-as-catch-can days; sometimes I barely remembered to feed my family. Most times, we were not even in town. Church, on the weekends when I wasn't speaking, became an agonizing event where I battled loneliness, exhaustion and tears. It was a wrestling match with my soul—and my kids—to show up.

This day, I went out of obedience. It was right, even with a heart scalded by the desert heat. Even if the children didn't want to go. Even if I had nothing to say to God beyond an anguished, "Help. Please."

Every song trumpeted God's faithfulness. And God began to woo me through the words, the melody, the fullness of the congregation's voice and faith. Even now, words fail to describe the effect of worship in the wilderness. As I focused on God, my problems and doubts lined up in front of me, and their weight dissipated like water sprinkled in a hot sauna. My perspective changed from my situation to God's watchful care, his capabilities, his power and, most of all, his love. For *me*. Fear seemed ridiculous. Worship that morning felt as if I just opened my heart and the Lord poured in his love and presence and peace. He soaked into each nook of my weary soul, not erasing all anxiety but rather presiding over it.

When we raise our hands to worship in the wilds of our life, God moves. It is inexplicable. But true. "Draw near to God and He will draw near to you" (James 4:9 NASB). When we turn toward our Lover, he turns toward us.

WORSHIP AND MOSES

In and about his daily work, Moses headed off with his sheep to the wilderness and came to "the mountain of God," Horeb. There he saw the angel of the Lord in the blazing bush that burned but wasn't consumed. Moses didn't try to talk himself out of seeing something miraculous ("It must be a mirage") or tell himself, "Hey, I don't have time for this! These sheep are stupid; I have work to do." He didn't holler, "Hold on, be there in a minute," the favored line of parents. Instead, he said, "I must turn aside now and see this marvelous sight, why the bush is not burned up" (Exodus 3:3 NASB).

And in his turning aside, in his pausing in his wilderness work, Moses encountered the living God, the God he'd spent forty years trying to grasp, the God who had delivered him from an angry king. Now deliverance came in another form, a deeper manner. Through worship, the burning heart of God took up residence in Moses' chest, and God's passion ignited him. He still had questions, but worship transformed the refugee-prince and murderer into a mighty leader.

THE WILDERNESS PATTERN

"Moses turned aside . . ." Turning aside to intersect with God would be the pattern for the desert. The Israelites' response: "When they heard that the LORD was concerned about them and had seen their misery, they bowed down and worshiped" (Exodus 4:31). What a prime reason for worship: God is concerned about us, sees our pain and loves us. How can we not love God in return? Sheer relief would lead us to worship.

The Jews later rejoiced in a canticle of praise at their escape from the terrorizing soldiers (Exodus 15). "And this shall be the sign to you that it is I who have sent you," God reassured Moses, "when you have brought the people out of Egypt, you shall worship God at this mountain" (Exodus 3:12 NASB). One of the first things God did after their safe escape was to establish a model for worship. He delivered the plans for the tabernacle, where they would meet with God regularly during their sojourn (Exodus 25).

Though still far from home, the Hebrews worshiped God, even with the blowing, gaunt unknown hitting them in the face like a hot wall of wind. Clearly the desert was no Promised Land and certainly no place to raise a family (of two million) and tend livestock. When they finally reached that mountain to worship, the people had no idea what freedom meant. They were safe from Egypt, but their freedom journey had just begun.

Even when we are not delivered from our transition trauma, we learn to turn to God in worship. Regardless of feeling, of the looming unknown, worship gives life in the barrens.

For the Israelites, worship in the wilderness was not optional. It was central to their desert experience. Choosing to turn our face toward God, bending our heart to bow before him whatever the circumstances, not only sustains us but also transforms us. Worship in the desert restores, renews and redirects our pilgrimage.

Like Moses, who turned aside, when we recognize God, we worship. And when we don't recognize God, we still worship the God we can't see.

WILDERNESS THEOLOGY

God's demand of Pharaoh holds for us, as well. "Let my people go, so that
they may worship me in the desert" (Exodus 7:16). All of life will conspire
to keep us from worship, but our
wilderness choice—our freedom
response in the desert—is to worship. Freedom begets worship, and
worship gives birth to freedom.

TRAVELOGUE

• *What has worship
been like for you—not Sunday in
the pew but worship from your
life, through your wilderness
experiences? Is it hard to
intersect God there?*

• *When has worship transported
you from the grime of problems
into holy space? What hinders
your worship in the desert?*

We give our anxieties far too
much attention and God far too
little. Reversing the system and re-
aligning our priorities diminishes
the anxiety. When we worship
God in spite of the evidence—that
our life is wrecked, that our neat
little world is swirling under the
advancing simoom—even though
it is the most countercultural form
of obedience we will muster, God
comes near.

In fact, this is one of the points
of worship: "Worship intends to
bring you into relationship with
the one who created you and gave
you life, who has provided for
your salvation, and who promises to stand with you forever. This is no
small purpose, or modest agenda." And it may just take a wilderness to
thrust us into that place of relationship, of dependence.

WHY WORSHIP?

Why worship in the near-desperation of the desert? God deserves it: we
direct our soul to God because of his glory. Not because our life is peachy

and perfect but because the One who loves us is holy, compassionate, all-powerful, present, wonderful, all-knowing. His hopes and dreams for us are beyond our most creative imaginings! We worship because in all the chaos and insanity of our life, our heart longs for Someone to hold us and guide us through the blind alleys of life. We have that Someone in our Savior. We sing with the psalmist, "Praise be to the Lord, to God our Savior, who daily bears our burdens" (Psalm 68:19).

Worship also brings perspective: the Scriptures tell us, "Be still, and know that I am God" (Psalm 46:10), and in worship we realize anew, *I can't be God here. I can't possibly figure this out.* We worship because of God's goodness to put us into a place of trust, where he can deliver.

TRAVELOGUE

• *What misgivings do you have about worship in the wilderness? Do you ever just feel angry at God for your situation? How do you resolve that tension without letting it separate you from him?*

• *When have you experienced praise bringing you into strength (Psalm 29)?*

Miraculously—here again, God does the paradox thing—we give and he gives back abundantly. Worship, according to the Scriptures, gives strength. Notice the order of Psalm 29: the writer says, "Ascribe to the LORD glory" (v. 1), and proceeding from that rightful praise, "the LORD gives strength to his people; the LORD blesses them with peace" (v. 11). In the paucity of the desert, praise is a secret to fullness (Psalm 63:1-8).

RESPONDING TO GRACE

In a recent journal entry, I moaned about my crowded life. Then I remembered a longing of the previous day to hear Jesus laugh. "Ah, Holy

Jesus, I think you have an infectious laugh that is like hot chocolate going down, warm and sweet and radiating. I can't wait to see you. I am so grateful that you love me. I have no words to speak of your life and death for me. You lived for me. You died for me. It hushes my heart, stills my anxious mind, fills me." And worship happened:

> I am grateful for the possibility of worship in the wilderness of our soul. You are above and beyond all our traumas and crises even while in the midst of them, and you direct our hearts outside—beyond the anguish to eternity. I am so glad that you are God, and that you will be exalted (Psalm 46:10). You are Lord of desert and mountaintop, sandstorm and anthill. Whether two million people are fleeing their captors or one woman is fighting for her life and heart in a world bent on destroying that heart— you are actively involved in rescue. Your interest in us never ends, you don't get tired of our neediness, and you are passionately after our hearts.

This is grace, and grace gets my heart. What a divine setup: God's goodness tethers us in the wilderness, and worship tethers us to God. Kathleen Norris writes:

> God will find a way to let us know that he is with us in this place, wherever we are, however far we think we've run. And maybe that's one reason we worship—to respond to grace. We praise God not to celebrate our own faith but to give thanks for the faith God has in us. To let ourselves look at God, and let God look back at us. And to laugh, and sing, and be delighted because God has called us his own.

That worship results in God's looking back at us in delight makes me smile. How can that be? How good of him to love us. Praising God expands our heart like aerobics for the soul. C. S. Lewis reminds us that worship is good practice for high and low times.

We—or at least I—shall not be able to adore God on the highest occasions if we have learned no habit of doing so on the lowest. At best, our faith and reason will tell us that He is adorable, but we shall not have found Him so, not have "tasted and seen." Any patch of sunlight in a wood will show you something about the sun that you could never get from reading books on astronomy. These pure and spontaneous pleasures are "patches of godlight" in the woods of experience.

Whether woods or wilderness, to not worship is deadly. "We die on the day when our lives cease to be illumined by the steady radiance of a wonder, the source of which is beyond all reason," said Dag Hammarskjöld. Without worship, the wilderness will suck the life out of us. The desert will win.

MOVING INTO WORSHIP

Do you remember Job's words in the midst of the biggest calamity of his life? His family is dead, his fortune is gone, his home is wiped out. "Then Job arose and tore his robe and shaved his head, and he fell to the ground and worshiped. . . . 'The LORD gave and the LORD has taken away. Blessed be the name of the LORD'" (Job 1:20-21 NASB).

TRAVELOGUE

• *Think of highs in your life where praise and worship came easily. Now remember the troughs where melody no longer sang in your heart. How did you find your way back to God?*

Where does such faith originate? My heart trembles at his words: "You are Lord. I will praise you regardless." Could I really worship God in such sweeping loss?

Nancy's second child was born with Zellweger's Syndrome, a rare metabolic and congenital disorder. Doctors gave Hope less than six months to live. While writing the book *Holding On to Hope,* where she processed their sorrow and sought God's purposes for their daughter's brief life, she learned she was pregnant again, in spite of her husband's vasectomy. Gabriel was born with the same condition, living short of six months. Nancy details her journey through pain as she looks at Job's life. "When our skin is pricked by a thorn, what comes out is what is inside: blood. When our lives are pricked by difficulty, what comes out is what is inside. . . . What came out when Job was not just pricked, but pierced, was worship."

We store up worship with a glance toward God here, a whisper of love there, a thank-you, a breath of praise, a gaze at beauty. Before long, worship—looking at God through our throbbing—becomes a lifestyle. In the midst of pain, of uncertainty, of devastation, our heart has practiced praise, and we turn aside to worship.

Worship is our transition template, our faithful companion, our reminder, our heart-starter in the wilderness. "When the Jews were in exile, the Sabbath became their temple, their sanctuary in time. It traveled with them wherever they went, a movable feast, a holy of holies that faithfully accompanied them in adversity."

We worship, then, wherever we are in our journey: in the sanctuary pew, scanning the help wanted ads, walking to school, learning to walk again, waiting out a hospital stay, staying by a dying loved one's bedside or kneeling by the bed begging for God's intervention in another's life. Or just lying flat out in the sand. I do not say this blithely. Above all else, God longs for our heart, and what better place to give it than when we are desperate? "Come to me, come to me," Jesus pleads. "Let me carry you. Let me give you rest" (Matthew 11:28-30 paraphrased). *Worship* is just that coming; it is the *rest* that God offers. It is giving over everything that we are (Romans 12:1-2).

No wonder song springs up in worship. Garrison Keilor says, "Singing is a form of extravagance." It is extravagant, like throwing gold dust up into a sandstorm—and yet, somehow, God inhabits the praise of his people. Silence and thanksgiving are forms of worship. When we move, when we dance, when we lift our hands, when we pick flowers, when we laugh, we worship. We see God's beauty even in the desert, his love for us in the sunset's palette, in the brilliant night sky and in the infinite forms of wilderness life. Nothing is too small to escape his creative touch and neither are we. So we turn to him in praise and gratitude.

We turn, not in an attempt to manipulate God into making our path straight. Worship "helps us accept our situation as it is, whether or not he changes it," says Ruth Myers. "Continued praise helps us reach the place where we can say, 'Father, I don't want You to remove this problem until You've done all You want to do through it, in me and in others.'" As Ruth tells the story of her husband's death from cancer, she says, "He decided that, through praise, he would make his hospital room a special dwelling place for God. 'I'll be praising God for all eternity, but only during my brief time on earth can I bring Him joy through praising Him in the midst of pain.'"

Worship restores our hope, lightens our step and gives onlookers a glimpse of heaven. We worship because our Christ was

> despised and forsaken of men,
> A man of sorrows, and acquainted with grief; . . .
> Surely our griefs He Himself bore,
> And our sorrows He carried. (Isaiah 53:3-4 NASB)

We worship not because all is well but because all things shall be well. Someday. Saint Augustine wrote:

> Let us sing alleluia here on earth, while we still live in anxiety, so that we may sing it one day in heaven in full security. . . .We shall have no enemies in heaven, we shall never lose a friend. God's praises are sung both there and here, but here they are sung in anxiety, there in security; here they are sung by those destined to die, there, by those destined to live forever; here they are sung in hope, there in hope's fulfillment; here, they are sung by wayfarers, there, by those living in their own country. So then . . . let us sing now,

not in order to enjoy a life of leisure, but in order to lighten our labors. You should sing as wayfarers do—sing, but continue your journey. . . . Sing then, but keep going.

Long Journey

We are not home yet. We are not, as my grandparents said, "out of the woods." Or the wilds. Whatever our life stage or specific transition, more will come. But in our travels, as we celebrate the options available to us, even in pain and uncertainty; as we realize that God has provided for us to follow, to feast and fellowship, to find fun and not forget his great goodness throughout our days; as we choose to allow him to redeem our travails and embrace the freedom of our heart; as we learn what it means to be found in Christ in the midst of our darkness and to even flourish there . . . then our heart bows in worship to this Lord of the wilderness, this God for whom no detail is too trivial, this God who discerns our pain and has compassion on us.

And the road, though arduous, becomes an intersection with the God who provides, who infuses divine unmerited assistance in the midst of our earthly turmoil. A grace point. A gift.

The story is told of a man invited to a celebration for his best friend. With no car in those days, he had only his strong legs to get him over multiple mountains and many difficult paths to reach his friend's home. For many days he traveled, and he finally arrived, disheveled and tired but jubilant, at his destination. When his friend answered the door, the traveler placed the gift in his hand.

"You came! It's so wonderful to see you. Please, please, come in."

"No, I must return now." The traveler turned to go.

"Oh, but you have come so far, walked so long. It is too much for you to leave so soon. You have only just arrived," said the friend, humbled by the effort required of his guest to attend the party.

The traveler shook his head, smiling.

"The long journey is part of the gift."

Wilderness Response

ACCOMPANIMENT PSALM

O God, you are my God,
*   earnestly I seek you;*
my soul thirsts for you,
*   my body longs for you,*
in a dry and weary land
*   where there is no water.*

I have seen you in the sanctuary
*   and beheld your power and your glory.*
Because your love is better than life,
*   my lips will glorify you.*
I will praise you as long as I live,
*   and in your name I will lift up my hands.*
My soul will be satisfied as with the richest of foods;
*   with singing lips my mouth will praise you.*

On my bed I remember you;
*   I think of you through the watches of the night.*
Because you are my help,
*   I sing in the shadow of your wings. . . .*
*   your right hand upholds me.*

PSALM 63:1-8

DESERT READING

And the LORD said [to Moses], "I will cause all my goodness to pass in front of you. . . . There is a place near me where you may stand on a rock. When my glory passes by, I will put you in a cleft in the rock and cover you with my hand until I have passed by. Then I will remove my hand and you will see my back; but my face must not be seen." . . .

When Moses came down from Mt. Sinai with the two tablets of the Testimony in his hands, he was not aware that his face was radiant because he had spoken with the LORD.

EXODUS 33:19-23; 34:29

GUIDING SONG

Come, Thou Fount of Every Blessing

Come, Thou Fount of every blessing,
Tune my heart to sing Thy grace;
Streams of mercy, never ceasing,
Call for songs of loudest praise. . . .

Jesus sought me when a stranger,
Wandering from the fold of God;
He, to rescue me from danger,
Interposed His precious blood.

O to grace how great a debtor
Daily I'm constrained to be!
Let Thy goodness, like a fetter,
Bind my wandering heart to thee.

WORDS: ROBERT ROBINSON, 1758 (1 SAMUEL 7:12)
MUSIC: WYETH'S REPOSITORY OF SACRED MUSIC,
PART SECOND, 1813

REMEMBER YOUR JOURNEY

- Breathe in the Scripture: "When they heard that the LORD was concerned about them and had seen their misery, they bowed down and worshiped" (Exodus 4:31). Wait with God now, to feel his compassion.

- Draw to mind your journey thus far—the pain, the uncertainty, the loss. Now look at God, who looks back at you with delight.

NOTES

Chapter 2: Choosing to Feel

The movie *The Edge,* in which Anthony Hopkins' character makes this statement, was directed by Lee Tamahori (20th Century Fox, 1997).

Abba Poeman's thoughts on guides of the soul are found in her book *Sayings of the Desert Fathers* (London: Mowbray, 1981), p. 172. The text as it is quoted here appears in Roberta Bondi, "Traveling On," *Weavings* 6, no. 6 (1991).

The discussion of the intensity of the Israelite's groaning is taken from the NET Bible (Dallas: Biblical Studies Press, 1997), p. 141 <www.netbible.com>.

The definition of "cried out" is taken from *Strong's Concordance* (McLean, Va.: MacDonald, n.d.).

The discussion of God's active listening and the relationship of hearing, remembering and obeying comes from the NET Bible, p. 141.

For David Viscott's approach to mental health, see his book *Emotional Resilience: Simple Truths for Dealing with the Unfinished Business of Your Past* (New York: Crown, Harmony Books, 1996), p. 5.

Ken Gire talks about our communion with God in *Windows of the Soul* (Grand Rapids, Mich.: Zondervan, 1996), p. 194.

Anne Lamott's observation that we need to experience "that ocean of sadness in a naked and immediate way" is taken from her book *Traveling Mercies: Some Thoughts on Faith* (New York: Pantheon, 1999), pp. 68-69.

Chapter 4: Choosing to Find the Meaning

The comment that Jesus intends to push us "toward a promise we cannot yet see" is given by M. Craig Barnes in his book *When God Interrupts* (Downers Grove, Ill.: InterVarsity Press, 1996), p. 54.

The original source for the poem by Louis Evely is unknown.

Christopher Reeve's thoughts on our response to disaster are found in an essay by Roger Rosenblatt, "New Hopes, New Dreams," *Time,* August 26, 1996, p. 48.

For more information about "Second Home Ministries," e-mail Miriam at <gmkelm@aol.com>.

The prayer is found in Jan Meyers, *The Allure of Hope* (Colorado Springs: NavPress, 2001), pp. 118-19. The italics are in the original.

For more background on spiritual gifts, read 1 Corinthians 12, Romans 12:3-16 and Ephesians 4:11. Chapter eleven of my book *Quiet Places: A Woman's Guide to Personal Retreat* (Minneapolis: Bethany House, 1997) discusses this subject more thoroughly.

Nicholas Wolterstorff's thoughts on Christ's wounds are taken from his book *Lament for a Son* (Grand Rapids, Mich.: Eerdmans, 1987), p. 90, as quoted by Meyers in *Allure of Hope,* p. 169.

Henri J. M. Nouwen's insights on Christ's wounds are taken from *The Wounded Healer* (New York: Doubleday, Image Books, 1979), pp. 82-83.

Gary Thomas discusses the perilous situations the Lord leads us through in "Finding Fortitude: Discover How to Navigate Life with a Steadfast Spirit," *Discipleship Journal,* July/August 2002, p. 40.

Chapter 5: Choosing to Be Found

Brennan Manning's observation that "God's name is Mercy" is taken from his book *The Ragamuffin Gospel* (Sisters, Ore.: Multnomah, 1990, 2000), pp. 231-32.

Chapter 6: Choosing to Flourish

Karen Mains comments on the paradox that "our souls often flourish in parched and arid terrain" are from her book *Soul Alert: Thriving Spiritually as Aliens and Strangers in the World* (Wheaton, Ill.: Mainstay Church Resources, 2002), pp. 2-3.

The temptation to not really live for the duration of the desert is discussed poignantly by M. Manette Ansay in her book *Limbo* (New York: Morrow, 2001), p. 230.

For the ability of plant life to find water, see an online geology class sponsored by Radford College in Radford, Virginia. The text was created in November 1996 and modified in October 1997, and it can be accessed by searching Google: "Radford: Swoodwar." On the Radford site, bring up "desertscrubs," which will lead to <http://www.radford.edu/~swoodwar/CLASSES/GEOG235/biomes/desert/desert.html>.

The discussion of the view of contemplation held by Bernard of Clairvaux comes from David Hazard's book *Your Angels Guard My Steps: A 40-Day Journey in the Company of Bernard of Clairvaux* (Minneapolis: Bethany House, 1998), p. 22. The italics are Hazard's.

"Because I believe God's plans for me are better than I can plan for myself, rather than run away from the path he has set before me, I want to run toward it," says Nancy Guthrie in *Holding On to Hope: A Pathway Through Suffering to the Heart of God* (Wheaton, Ill.: Tyndale House, 2002), p. 88.

For the unexpected flowers and fragrances that appeared after the 1998 El Niño, see "In Full Bloom," *Vogue*, May 2001.

The Reverend Barbara Brown Taylor's statement that God's intention is to expand the breadth and depth of our life as opposed to meeting our idea of happiness is quoted in Jan Karon's book *Patches of Godlight: Father Tim's Favorite Quotes* (New York: Viking Penguin Putnam, 2001).

Chapter 7: Choosing to Focus

The hymnal I reviewed is *Praise! Our Songs and Hymns,* edited by John W. Peterson and Norman Johnson (Grand Rapids, Mich.: Zondervan, Singspiration Music, 1979). The categories are taken from the preface.

Eugene Peterson's rendering of Psalm 121:1-2 is from his translation of the Bible, *The Message: The Bible in Contemporary Language* (Colorado Springs: NavPress, 2002), p. 1069.

The "need to feel pain before you can accept it" and the danger of holding in our anger are discussed by Viscott in *Emotional Resilience,* p. 15.

The concept that Jesus "invited people further into their fears" rather than allowing them to skirt those fears is presented by Barnes in *When God Interrupts,* p. 21.

Chapter 8: Choosing to Feast

St. Augustine's observation that "longing is the heart's treasury" is quoted in John Eldredge, *Journey of Desire* (Nashville: Thomas Nelson, 2000), p. 53.

The author of this statement in the edition of *The Cloud of Unknowing* prepared by William Johnson (New York: Bantam Doubleday Dell, 1973), p. 46, is unknown.

The need to ask God "for bread for this day, not for all of them" is discussed by Dorothy C. Bass in *Receiving the Day: Christian Practices for Opening the Gift of Time* (San Francisco: Jossey-Bass, 2000), p. 25.

Some of the books on suffering, mercy and grace which Gretchen and David found helpful include Philip Yancey, *Where Is God When It Hurts?* (Grand Rapids, Mich.: Zondervan, 1996); Richard Chilson, *You Shall Not Want: A Spiritual Journey Based on the Psalms* (Notre Dame, Ind.: Ave Maria Press, 1996) and books by Evelyn Underhill.

Eugene Peterson's thoughts on the need to integrate human effort into "the rhythms of grace and blessing" appear in his book *Working the Angles: The Shape of Pastoral Integrity* (Grand Rapids, Mich.: Eerdmans, 1987), p. 69, and are given as quoted in *Receiving the Day,* p. 18.

Simone Weil's observation that only by lying can the soul "persuade itself that it is not hungry" is quoted in Eldredge, *Journey of Desire,* p. 15.

Calvin Miller's thoughts on emptiness are taken from his book *Into the Depths of God* (Minneapolis: Bethany House, 2000), p. 28.

Chapter 9: Choosing Spiritual Friendship

David Benner's observation that "intimate relationships prepare us for intimacy with God" appears in his book *Sacred Companions: The Gift of Spiritual Friendship and Direction* (Downers Grove, Ill.: InterVarsity Press, 2002), p. 41.

C. S. Lewis's insights on the basis of lifelong friendships are given as quoted in *The Hungry Souls Newsletter,* November 2002.

Fyodor Dostoyevsky's famous comment on love, found in *The Brothers Karamazov,* trans. Richard Pevear and Larissa Volokhonsky (New York: Knopf, 1992), p. 320, is quoted in Meyers, *Allure of Hope,* p. 77.

Dietrich Bonhoeffer's observation that "it is God's love for us that he not only gives us his Word but also lends us his ear" appears in his book *Life Together;* here it is quoted in "Finding Friendship in an Unlikely Place," *Focus on the Family,* November 2000, p. 16.

Thomas Merton's thoughts on overcoming the fear of not being loved come from his book *No Man Is an Island* (London: Harvest, Harcourt Brace Jovanovich, 1983), p. 202, as quoted in Meyers, *Allure of Hope*, p. 77.

Douglas D. Webster's thoughts on broken relationships as a source of pain in our culture appear in *Soulcraft: How God Shapes Us Through Relationships* (Downers Grove, Ill.: InterVarsity Press, 1999), p. 15.

Henri J. M. Nouwen's comments on the desert as being the "vast empty space where the God of love reveals himself and offers his promise to those who are waiting in faithfulness" are from his book *The Genesee Diary* (New York: Bantam Doubleday Dell, Image Books, 1976), p. 69.

Ronald E. Wilson discusses community in his book *Stretching the Soul* (Grand Rapids, Mich.: Revell, 1995), p. 19.

Imagine a friend singing "Wonderful Words of Life" to you, calling you to life and faith.

Chapter 10: Choosing to Find Fun

Patch's digression on laughter, which appears in the film *Patch Adams,* starring Robin Williams, Monica Potter and Daniel London (Universal Studios, 1998), is quoted in Shirley Mitchell's book *Fabulous After 50* (Green Forest, Ark.: New Leaf, 2000), p. 43.

Chapter 11: Choosing to Not Forget

Jan Meyers's thoughts on the value of our stories appear in her book *Allure of Hope,* p. 110.

For more information about Christian Youth Theater, or to find a chapter near you, visit <www.cctcyt.org> or call 1-800-696-1929.

Chapter 12: Choosing Freedom

Ann Peacock wrote the screenplay for the 1999 film *A Lesson Before Dying.* Robert Benedette was the producer; Joseph Sargent, the director. The film was based on the novel by Ernest J. Gaines (New York: Vintage, 1994).

For *liberty,* see *Webster's Collegiate Dictionary* (Springfield, Mass.: G & C Merriam, 1977).

Chapter 13: Worship in Transition's Wilderness

John Buchanan comments on the role of worship in our relationship with our Creator and Savior in *reNEWS: A Publication of Presbyterians for Renewal,* February 1993, p. 6.

The observation that "we praise God not to celebrate our own faith but to give thanks for the faith God has in us" appears in Kathleen Norris's book *Amazing Grace: A Vocabulary of Faith* (New York: Riverhead, 1998), p. 151.

The observation that we "shall not be able to adore God on the highest occasions if we have learned no habit of doing so on the lowest" comes from C. S. Lewis, *Letters to Malcolm: Chiefly on Prayer,* as quoted in Karon, *Patches of Godlight.*

Dag Hammarskjöld's thoughts are given as quoted in Buchanan, *reNEWS,* p. 7.

"What came out when Job was not just pricked, but pierced, was worship," says Nancy Guthrie in her book *Holding On to Hope,* p. 18.

Wayne Muller's comments on the Sabbath as a temple for the Jews appear in *Sabbath: Restoring the Sacred Rhythm of Rest* (New York: Bantam, 1999), p. 36.

Ruth Meyers's thoughts on prayer in the midst of suffering come from her book *31 Days to Praise* (Sisters, Ore.: Multnomah, 1994), pp. 121-22

St. Augustine's observation that we "sing alleluia here on earth, while we still live in anxiety, so that we may sing it one day in heaven in full security" is quoted in Kathleen Norris, *Amazing Grace,* p. 368.

BIOGRAPHICAL INFORMATION

*K*nown for her vulnerability, spiritual depth and humor, Jane Rubietta is a popular and frequent keynote speaker at events around the continent. Among other books, she has written *Quiet Places* (Bethany House) and *How to Keep the Pastor You Love* (IVP). She and her husband, Rich, have founded the not-for-profit Abounding Ministries, whose mission is to offer people a life-changing experience of God's love in Jesus Christ through music, writing, speaking and retreats in communities, schools and churches. For more information, contact:

Jane Rubietta
Abounding Ministries
225 Bluff Avenue
Grayslake, IL 60030
847-223-4790
www.abounding.org
jrubietta@abounding.org

If your church, women's ministry or special events coordinator is interested in considering Jane for a conference, retreat, banquet or training event, please contact SpeakUp! Speaker Services toll-free at 888-870-7719 or e-mail at <Speakupinc@aol.com>. Visit them online at <www.SpeakUpSpeakerServices.com>.